Routledge Revivals

The Malays

First published in 1961, *The Malays* reveals the Malay as the inheritor of an ancient and complex civilization made up of Mongolian shamanism; Assyrio-Babylonian and Tantric magic; art motifs from the steppes; Dong-so'n and India; the religions, folklore and literature of Buddhist, Hindu and Muslim; the laws of a peasantry who abandoned democracy for the feudal role of Hindu Rajas, the earthly incarnations of Indra. There are chapters dealing with the origin of the Malays and their descent from Yunnan, their social, political, legal and economic systems, their beliefs and religions and arts and crafts. This book should be of value to all interested in history, art and the culture of India and of the Far East and to all students of Islam.

The Malays
A Cultural History

R. O. Winstedt

First published in 1947
Second edition (revised) 1950
Third edition 1953
Fourth edition 1956
Fifth edition 1958
Sixth edition (with some corrections) 1961
By Routledge & Kegan Paul Ltd.

This edition first published in 2024 by Routledge
4 Park Square, Milton Park, Abingdon, Oxon, OX14 4RN
and by Routledge
605 Third Avenue, New York, NY 10017

Routledge is an imprint of the Taylor & Francis Group, an informa business

© Richard Winstedt, 1961

All rights reserved. No part of this book may be reprinted or reproduced or utilised in any form or by any electronic, mechanical, or other means, now known or hereafter invented, including photocopying and recording, or in any information storage or retrieval system, without permission in writing from the publishers.

Publisher's Note
The publisher has gone to great lengths to ensure the quality of this reprint but points out that some imperfections in the original copies may be apparent.

Disclaimer
The publisher has made every effort to trace copyright holders and welcomes correspondence from those they have been unable to contact.

A Library of Congress record exists under LCCN: 50014932

ISBN: 978-1-032-73304-3 (hbk)
ISBN: 978-1-003-46372-6 (ebk)
ISBN: 978-1-032-73338-8 (pbk)

Book DOI 10.4324/9781003463726

A Malay Girl planting Rice

[*Frontispiece*

THE MALAYS
A CULTURAL HISTORY

by

RICHARD WINSTEDT

K.B.E., C.M.G., F.B.A., D.LITT.,
HON. LL.D. (MALAYA)

ROUTLEDGE & KEGAN PAUL LTD
Broadway House, 68–74 Carter Lane
London, E.C.4.

First published 1947
Second edition (revised) 1950
Third edition 1953
Fourth edition 1956
Fifth edition 1958
Sixth edition (with some corrections) 1961
Corrections © *Richard Winstedt* 1961

PRINTED IN GREAT BRITAIN BY
LOWE AND BRYDONE (PRINTERS) LTD., LONDON, N.W.10

CONTENTS

		PAGE
	Foreword	vii
1.	Introduction	1
2.	Origin, Migrations and Language	5
3.	Beliefs and Religion	18
4.	Social Systems	45
5.	Political Systems	63
6.	Legal Systems	91
7.	Economic Systems	120
8.	Literature	139
9.	Arts and Crafts	161
10.	The Future	176
11.	Appendices:—	
	(a) Malay Text of Passages Cited in the Chapters	182
	(b) Relationships in Negri Sembilan	187
	Bibliography	191
	Index	197

ILLUSTRATIONS

	PAGE
A Malay Girl Planting Rice	*Front*
Malay Children Fishing in a Rice-Swamp	12
Malay Weapons	48
A Kedah Market	80
Fishermen, Trengganu	122
In the Market, Kuala Trengganu	134
A Trengganu Fishing Boat	160
Malay Silver-Work and a Gold Waist-Buckle	172

FOREWORD

THIS IS a revised and enlarged edition of a work originally published in Singapore.

On some of the subjects handled in it hitherto only scattered and fragmentary notes have been printed. Of Malay industries only one has been adequately described, and that recently by Professor Raymond Firth in his book on *Malay Fishermen: their Peasant Economy*. Much has been written on the matriarchy of Negri Sembilan, but to have made my chapter longer would have thrown it out of focus. On Malay beliefs and Malay literature I have written separate volumes, but here again available material has been condensed not to distort the general picture.

Only in the chapter on Arts and Crafts have I gone in some paragraphs outside Malaya to the archipelago for the sake of perspective.

Two Appendices have been added, one for those interested in the Malay language, the other for those interested in the Minangkabau matriarchy.

I am indebted to Professor Raymond Firth for the plates facing pages 12 and 80 and to Mr. C. A. Gibson-Hill for all the other illustrations except the two on Malay Weapons and Malay Silver-work, for which I have to thank the authorities of the Victoria and Albert Museum.

London, 1953   R.O.W.

In this fifth edition opportunity has been taken to revise some details in the light of recent research.

London, 1958   R.O.W.

1: INTRODUCTION

THE conception of culture in this book is implicit in its table of contents. Broadly it is regarded as a body of ideas, practices and techniques that have been cherished by the Malays long enough to affect their way of life, a legacy that gives them heart and interests and saves their minds from inanition as food saves their bodies. Malay culture includes a fear of nature spirits, an instinctive perception of the "unbecoming" rather than of the sinful and the criminal, the *séance* of the shaman, the Hindu ritual of a royal installation, the celebration of the Muhammadan New Year, the sermon in the mosque, the pilgrimage to Mecca, Sufi mysticism, the Hamlet of the Malay opera, the curry, football, the cinema and the mistranslations of the vernacular press. It includes, indeed, much more, but compared with the (comparatively few) great cultures of the world it has been derivative, owing ideas and practices to prehistoric influences of central Asia, to the kingship and architecture of Assyria and Babylon, to bronze-workers and weavers from Indo-China, to the religions and arts and literature of India, to the religion and literature of Persia and Arabia, to the material civilisations of Portugal, Holland and Great Britain and to the remote but compelling fantasies of Hollywood. Many of the more primitive beliefs of the Malay survive to-day only in sequestered hamlets or in the customs of such backward tribes as the Torajas of Celebes or the Igorots of Luzon. Many are mere survivals in culture like our avoidance of ladders or our dislike of spilling salt or having thirteen at a table.

A faculty that has always made for the Malay's progress has been his power to accept the new and adjust it to the old. So, from fear of local spirits and godlings he passed through acceptance of the Hindu pantheon to the worship of Allah, the One God. In prehistoric days, for example, he shared Asia's wide-spread belief in a Spectre Huntsman, whom Aryans came to identify with a storm-god, Rudra, and

Hindus with Siva. The Malays not only identified their Spectre Huntsman with Siva when they became Hindus, but on conversion to Islam they identified both the Spectre Huntsman and Siva with the father of Islam's djinns. Obviously such syncretism avoided any serious break in tradition and satisfied racial and intellectual pride.

Perhaps it was the stir of the Aryan migration that carried to the Malays in Yunnan the Assyrio-Babylonian practices which are the earliest of their cultural loans that can be identified. To-day the only one of them accepted and adapted by Islam is the magician's incantation, and even this is doomed with the advent of science and of a higher conception of prayer. Malay culture no longer respects the number seven as comprising sun and moon and the five planets. A more rational view of life combined with Islamic fatalism has left divination from the flight of birds and from the livers of animals to jungle folk like the Dayaks. The pyramid of the Near East profoundly affected the architecture of the Javanese even when they had become Hindus, but its inspiration was religious, and when Islam condemned architecture and painting infected with polytheism, the culture of the civilized Malay practically ceased to include art; none of the Minangkabau colonists of Negri Sembilan have houses carved and painted like those of their Sumatran home-land.

Another religious feature of Assyrio-Babylonian culture was the notion of "the right divine of kings to govern wrong". It was easy, therefore, for the Malay to accept kings as incarnations of Indra or Vishnu, until Islam reduced them to be no more than descendants of Alexander the Great. But the old halo of divinity crowned Malay rulers until in quite recent times it has been impaired by democratic and communist doctrines.

For more than five hundred years Islam has integrated Malay culture. In theory the Malay has no ideals of truth, beauty or goodness that lie outside the tenets of his faith, though in fact those ideals are encrusted with the debris of earlier beliefs and are being transformed, however gradually, by the non-sectarian altruism and secular humanism of the West.

The knell of theocratic culture, that started to totter in Europe two centuries ago, is sounding now in a Malay world, where religion and politics are beginning to be conceived as separate activities. Before the Japanese war the passing of the old order was almost imperceptible. Mecca was (and is still) the spiritual home of the religious, and Malay secular authors have owed more to Cairo than to an English education. But insensibly European influence envelopes the Malay. For the many its main contributions have been the three R's, football, the cinema and khaki clothes. The few it is transmuting into a new middle class with foreign ideals. And though at this time European and American and Communist ideals centre round an earthly paradise that can never be realized, they are at least of temporary value to the Malay, whose need of economic betterment is great. Similarly the modern insistence on human rights rather than social duties is at the moment of political value to him. But it must not be forgotten that the Malay was acquainted with democracy and electorates several thousand years ago, till the coastal tribes turned away to accept Hindu aristocracy and kingship. Even the Malays of Minangkabau who stuck by the older way of government did not find it enough to give them spiritual satisfaction, hedged though it was with primitive religious sanctions; they, too, accepted Hindu kings who were deities incarnate. Today democracy is in the ascendant, being confused often with nationalism.

Of recent years the Malay is sometimes called an Indonesian. Employed first in 1850 by J. R. Logan of Penang, the noun Indonesia covered the island world of Netherlands India and the Philippines. Adopted by philologists, the adjective Indonesian came to denote the languages of Indonesia, Malaya, the Mergui archipelago and

Formosa and of tribes in Indo-China and Madagascar. Anthropologists use it to denote the racial strain (predominant in Batak and Dayak) which along with a Mongoloid element made up the Proto-Malay. Finally the term has proved acceptable to politicians of races despised by the more advanced peoples of the Malay archipelago and so has come to be employed as a general term for all the races of that region.

Less confusing is the connotation of the term Malay, which denotes more particularly the civilized Malays of Sumatra and the Malay peninsula and in a broader sense almost all the inhabitants of the Malay archipelago, Formosa and the Philippines and some of the tribes of Indo-China. The word Malay as a noun is employed to denote persons or language. The word Malaya for the peninsula is of European invention. The term Malayan denotes any inhabitant of that peninsula, Asian or European.

2: ORIGIN, MIGRATION AND LANGUAGE

THE remote ancestral background of the Malay has to be constructed from skulls and palaeoliths excavated in Mongolia and at Pekin and from the river terraces of Java, and it has to be corroborated for later centuries by study of the neoliths and extant primitive tribes of the Malay world. From the beginning of the Pleistocene (or Ice Age) about one million years ago, when the Malay peninsula became linked with Java, Sumatra and Borneo, the mandibles of two giant forerunners of man have survived, namely those of the Java Giant (*Pithecanthropus palaeojavanicus*) with a head as large as that of an adult male gorilla and the Ape-Man of Modjokerto (*Pithecanthropus modjokertensis* or *robustus*). From the Middle Pleistocene date the remains of Java's famous *Pithecanthropus erectus*), the erect forerunner of Neanderthal man, found at solo along with the remains of a primitive elephant, a *Stegodon*, a hippopotamus, a *Cryptomastodon* and two species of rhinoceros. Later still from the beginning of the Upper Pleistocene come eleven skull-caps and two thigh-bones of a larger and more highly developed pithecanthropoid, the Man from Solo (*Homo Soloensis*), who camped on river-banks and used rough stone implements of yellow chalcedony, a cannibal apparently who split the skulls of his victims. He is no longer accompanied by the *Stegodon*, the elephant, the hippopotamus and the antelope but a prehistoric Gaur and water-buffalo abound in his vicinity. Finally, there is the man from Wajak (*Homo wadjakensis*), claimed as the ancestor of an Australvid skull from Keilor, near Melbourne. Though still larger than any man today, the Wajak man yet has the teeth of *Homo Sapiens*

The most ancient implements unearthed in the Malay peninsula are those from Kota Tampan in the Perak valley, large heavy pebble artifacts of the chopper type, usually flaked on one side only, that appear to have affinity with similar artifacts from Pleistocene terraces in India, Burma and Java. Some of the gravels from which the

Perak artifacts were taken "underlie a deposit of volcanic tuff, probably derived from the eruption that formed the crater now occupied by the Toba lake in Sumatra". Conclusive evidence is still needed to support the view that the earliest chopping tools of Burma, Perak and Java represent the culture of men of the type of China's *Sinanthropus pekinensis* and Java's *Pithecanthropus erectus*.

When we come to the later mesolithic cultures of the Malay world, then the caves and rock-shelters of limestone hills in Kedah, Kelantan, Perak and Pahang provide ample material, practically all suitable sites appearing to have been inhabited. The term mesolithic, it must be explained, is not used by the prehistorians of south-east Asia to denote an intermediate link in the evolution of stone artifacts from the flaked hand-axe of the Pleistocene period to the polished quadrangular neolith and cord-marked pottery of the last four thousand years of Indonesian (or Malay) culture. These mixed mesolithic cultures are late palaeolithic cultures more or less affected and transformed by subsequent and foreign neolithic influences from the north. They are commonly called Hoabinhian or Bacsonian or Bacson-Hoabinhian after places in Indo-China where they were found in large numbers. In Indo-China and in Malaya skeletal remains occurring with the flaked hand-axes or scrapers of this culture belong to the Australo-Melanesoid racial group. And probably some at least of these people who left their rough implements in the Yangtze gorges, Siam, Sumatra, Java, the Philippines, Celebes and Australia were ancestors of the Australian aborigine and the Melanesian of to-day. Study of a lower jaw from a shell-heap at Guak Kepah (in Province Wellesley) has led a Dutch anthropologist to surmise that the ancestors of those two groups, namely the Australoids and Melanesoids, were already differentiated before leaving the continent of Asia. Before passing down through the Malay archipelago they left some 7,000 years ago their chipped hand-axe or scraper, their grinding-stones and ruddle along with the shells of the molluscs and the bones of the animals they ate, in the caves of northern Malaya and the shell-heaps of Province Wellesley, and their physical characteristics in Malaya's jungle tribes.

Is it mere coincidence, one wonders, that there is the closest resemblance between the elaborate Malay belief in a soul-substance (*semangat*), possessed by all things, man alive or dead, his hair, teeth and nails, beasts, trees, rice, stones, weapons, houses and boats, and the Melanesian belief in *mana*, an impersonal power attached to men, animals, fruits, stones, canoes and water and responsible for the success and failure of men and crops? Among Australia's aborigines, in Melanesia, Polynesia, the Andaman Islands and the Malay archipelago the head especially is revered as being possessed of valuable soul-substance; the heads of ancestors are kept by Melanesians and Polynesians, while the Solomon Islander and the Dayak of Borneo and the Torajas of Celebes to ensure health and good crops would add the heads of slain enemies or murdered strangers to their grisly collection of soul-full skulls.[1] A common source for the beliefs of both racial groups or an Indonesian debt to the ancestors of the Melanesian for this belief in soul-substance would hardly be surprising, seeing that in the caves of Tonkin and Perak there have been found both Melanesoid and Indonesian skulls.

Traces of the ancestors of the Australian and Melanesian survive in Malaya in the skulls and beards of some of its jungle-folk. Including such traces these people reveal four or five racial types, but they may be conveniently divided into three main groups: (1) the Negrito, (2) the Senoi (or Sakai), classed by some as Veddoid but generally as Indonesian, and (3) Jakun or Proto-Malay or Mongoloid Indonesian. The scientist, however, so far from viewing them as pure and unmixed groups, will prefer to regard one

[1] Heads fixed on the branches of a village tree of death are still a common pattern on cloths from Sumba Island.

as predominantly Negrito and another as predominantly Indonesian, especially as in all three there occur those older strata, Australoid and Melanesoid.

The oldest of Malaya's existing races anthropologically is the Negrito, termed Semang in Perak and Pangan in Kelantan, a brownish-black curly-haired pigmy, generally short-skulled, a relative of the Aetas of the Philippines and the Mincopies of the Andaman islands and thought to contribute an element in the peoples of Indo-China, Malaya, the Malay archipelago, New Guinea and (British) India, though that element may perhaps be Melanesoid. Malaya's 3,000 Negrito nomads have not braved the fastnesses of the hill-tribes but have kept to the west coast from Trang to the Dindings and have skirted the foot of the main range through Upper Perak Kelantan Trengganu and Pahang. Neither in Indo-China nor in Malaya do their skeletal remains occur before the neolithic period. They build neither boats, rafts nor houses but sleep in rock or tree shelters or on a floor of sticks under a wall-less leaf-shelter propped on a stick and hardly bigger than a chicken hutch. Their diet consists of jungle fruits and roots and a little wild game and fish. In the Philippines they used the bow and arrow as they once did in Malaya, though now they have borrowed the blow-pipe of the Senoi. They fear thunder and lightning and propitiate this terrific power by cutting their shins and offering the blood. They believe in kindly elves who live in flowers. Like the Andaman Islander, the Melanesian, the Senoi and the Proto-Malay, they think there is an island for the dead with fruit-laden trees, to be reached over a narrow tree-trunk; Senoi describe it as a rainbow-snake and negritos of Kelantan say, only a shaman helped by tree-burial can fly over the head of its demon guardian. It is a primitive belief shared by Indonesian, Turki and Mongol pagans and may have been brought by a Tokharian migration from Europe before 720 B.C.

In the wavy-haired cinnamon-coloured Senoi have been detected Australoid and Veddoid strains (the latter from Ceylon and southern India) but in the main the Senoi (or

Sakai) is an Indonesian, kinsman of the Bataks of Sumatra and the Dayaks of Borneo and many hill-folk in south China, Indo-China and the Malay archipelago. Taller than the Negrito and often refined in features, the Senoi hillmen of Malaya number some 24,000 persons. Their faces are adorned with painted patterns and the septum of the nose is often perforated for the insertion of bone, wood or quill. The ears of the women are similarly perforated and adorned. They plant rice and millet, tapioca, sweet potatoes, sugar-cane and a little tobacco. Their houses are always built on piles and often communal. The Senoi is an artist in bamboo. His weapon is the blow-pipe, common throughout the Indonesian world, a long hollow bamboo or wooden tube from which is blown a tiny dart tinged with vegetable poison. His tools, till he got iron from civilised neighbours, must have been bamboo slivers and for heavier work the Indonesian polished quadrate adze so plentiful throughout Malaya.

The Senoi language, like Senoi culture, must have been Indonesian but was swamped by a large admixture of Mon-Annam, spoken by perhaps two waves of immigrants who followed the Senoi into Malaya. The last wave carried Mon numerals up to ten to the aborigines upon a line running up the Lebir river in Kelantan, along the Tembeling into Pahang as far as Tasek Bra and thence westward across the peninsula by way of the Serting and the Palong to an area just north of Muar. One of the offshoots of this line is Kenaboi mountain in Jelebu, where two bronze socketted axe-heads were discovered in tin-mines. This type of celt, unknown to India and the Near East, came from Europe to Asia to be carried south along with *motifs* surviving in Batak art and Sumba cloths and with bronze-drums, like the two whose fragments were found in the Tembeling and at Klang. This culture is called after Dong-so'n, from the results of excavations at that place in North Annam. Apparently it was distributed by ancestors of the Annamites, Yue traders from Indo-China. These people must have reached Malaya not earlier than 500 B.C. or later than the time of Christ. The presence of a small bronze bowl beside a stone cist, found in Batang Padang, suggests that its builders were the carriers of this Dong-so'n culture, and the same people may have been the miners who dug large pits ascribed by modern Malays to the Siamese. As far away as Celebes a neolithic *cache* was found containing pottery decorated with incised patterns of triangles, zigzag lines, wavy lines, spirals and stylized human figures related to the patterns of this Indo-Chinese bronze-age. Except for the descent of the Thai in historical times this movement of Indo-Chinese speaking a Mon-Annam language was the last of the migrations southward from central Asia.

Most important of all the migrations was that of Mongoloid Indonesian or Proto-Malay. Apart from Polynesia with its Indonesian affinities the Malay world covers the peninsula of Malacca as it is still called on the continent, most of Indonesia, the Philippines and Formosa. The peoples of Malay race are now sixty millions in number.

The hunters and food-gatherers of the mesolithic period had lived many of them in caves and rock-shelters easy to locate and explore. But the Indonesians of the neolithic period were agriculturists whose villages are discovered only by some accident like the great flood of 1926 that revealed one at Tembeling in Pahang. The most valuable *cache* so far explored was not in the west, but the Celebes *cache*, which revealed violin-shaped stone tools resembling those of the neolithic of Japan and polished stone arrow-heads related to those of Japan, Manchuria and China. As no stone arrow-heads occur in Indo-China, Siam, Malaya and Sumatra, those from Celebes and eastern Java may have come from Japan by way of the Philippines. There are many neolithic workshops in Java indicating a large population, and one workshop has been found in Sumatra. The adzes and gouges from Java and south Sumatra are often made from agate jasper and chalcedony, presumably for the ceremonial purposes of an advanced civilization. But the migration of these neolithic peoples from the continent of Asia took place before the development of a tanged adze introduced by Mongoloid peoples from Assam or Burma to the Mongoloid Mundas of Orissa and Chota Nagpur, since except in Celebes the tanged adze common in Burma, Siam and Indo-China never reached the southern half of Malaya or the Malay archipelago. Its introduction into India must have preceded the Aryan invasion. On this evidence Dr. Heine-Geldern and Dr. Van Stein Callenfels put the Malay migration from Asia between 2500 and 1500 B.C. Their quadrangular adze culture accompanied by unglazed cordmarked pottery of great variety has been traced from China southward, and Dr. Heine-Geldern thinks that the development of "highly specialized pick-adzes" of Java and Sumatra, "from a simple adze-type with quadrangular cross-section and semi-circular edge found in Laos, through an intermediate type frequent in Malaya clearly indicates the direction and way of the ancient migration". Reaching the coast these peoples, who were to carry the quadrangular adze and the Malay language family so far, crossed to the archipelago in outrigger craft developed from bamboo outriggers still in use on many rivers of Burma and Indo-China. In this craft they voyaged as far as Easter Island and Madagascar. And early in the Christian era they colonized Polynesia.

As language and prehistorian research show, these ancestors of the Malays, while still living on the continent of Asia, cultivated the banana, sugarcane and cucumbers and were acquainted with bamboo and the coconut. They planted millet and rice, using a tiny knife for reaping so as not to frighten the rice-soul, a knife whose stone prototype has been traced in Tonkin. They brewed beer from rice or millet. They had domesticated the pig, the buffalo and probably cattle. They were fishermen as well as hunters, with lobsters, prawns and turtle as part of their fare. Their clothes were of bark. They were head-hunters, living in houses on piles constructed of bamboo and wood with rattan lashings. They could count up to a thousand and possessed some knowledge of astronomy. They made pottery. And they were builders of megaliths. Without much risk of error one may supplement this picture by comparing the life and customs of the civilized Malay of yesterday with those of the Khassis of Assam, another people with an Indonesian element in their language, who ceased to be in touch with Indonesians more than 3000 years ago.

By the Malay and by the Khassi the umbilical cord is cut with a bamboo knife and the placenta are preserved for some days. To both races it is tabu to reap rice with a sickle. The spring-gun impelling an arrow, pitfalls with bamboo caltrops at the bottom, nooses for roping deer, a concealed platform that sinks under the weight of an animal and releases a roof weighted with stones that crushes the beast beneath, bird-snares of bamboo limed with the gum of the jack-tree—all these are common to both races. *Tuba* is used for fishing by the Khassi and by the Malay. Children of both races fly kites. Neither race till recently had the potter's wheel. Neither race cares for butter, ghee or milk—unless the last is imported in tins. Like the Chinese and Dayak, both races used the cock for sacrifices. Both employed ordeal by water. Some of these articles and practices may have come into being independently and others may be the borrowings of later ages. But there is no doubt that added together they give a fair picture of the Proto-Malay before he left the continent of Asia.

So, too, will comparison of the culture of the Malay with that of the Mois of Indo-China, an Indonesian people from whom the Malay has been parted for several thousand years. The games of their children are similar, and so are their traps and snares. Both employed ordeal by water and by boiling resin. Among both debt slavery was common. The similarity of their beliefs and superstitions is striking but these belong to a later chapter.

Shamanism was the religion of Ural-Altaic peoples from the Behring Straits to Scandinavia, and of the early Mongols.

Malay Children fishing in a Rice-Swamp

[*face p. 12*

The Pro-Malays are a blend of early Mongol and Indonesian. In Malaya to-day they are represented by 7000 Jakun, who live in the forests of Pahang and Johor. The original home of the race had long been traced on linguistic grounds to Indo-China but more recently cultural evidence has pointed to the north-west of Yun-nan. Like Malaya's other aborigines they must have got the shaman's *séance* and his association with were-tigers (Asia's counterpart to lycanthropy) from contact with early Mongols who trekked south to Tibet, Yun-nan and beyond. Not one of Malaya's aboriginal peoples buried a shaman: they would expose his corpse either in a tree or in the forest or on a platform, so that his spirit might escape aloft, as some think, helped by the rending claws of a dead shaman ancestor in tiger form. The Sea Dayaks suspended the body of a shaman from a tree. In Mongolia "shamans are generally buried on elevated places or in the crossways".

One might think it was from the Mongoloid element in his make-up that the Proto-Malay inherited his elaborate care for the dead, from whom the Senoi flee in terror. But it is rash to generalize when ancient bronze drums depict lavish Dayak funeral ceremonies connected, it would appear, with the civilization of Dong-so'nian bronze-workers. Anyhow close to the grave of a Besisi (a Proto-Malay tribe settled in Malacca and Selangor) a temporary hut is built and furnished for man or woman, as the case may be, with inclined stick-ladders to enable the soul of the deceased to climb into it. A Proto-Malay chief who died in 1879 had a grave with several Muslim characteristics but also with a ditch round the mound in which his spirit could paddle a ghostly canoe, and with small upright sticks called soul-ladders to enable the spirit to quit the grave at will. At the foot of some Jakun graves the soul-ladder is said to be 5 feet tall and to have 14 notches. The Indonesian Dayak also used a notched stick-ladder fixed upside down in the path near a cemetery to stop departed spirits from straying to the danger of the public. It is particularly difficult to try to isolate Proto-Malay customs and beliefs because the modern representative of the Proto-Malay is so quick to lap suggestions from his neighbours. A Jakun (or Proto-Malay) marriage ceremony, for example, requires the groom to walk or run after his bride three or seven times round a hillock, a ritual perhaps symbolic of capture combined with the circumambulation common in Hindu ceremonial. For the pagan Jakun kept touch with the mediaeval science of the civilised Malay, and learnt to invoke Hindu deities and Allah and His Prophet in their charms. They will placate ghosts of the dead, the spirits of all diseases and innumerable spirits of river and forest, the spirits of tigers, monkeys and even elephants, the spirits of eaglewood, of the camphor-tree, the wild rubber-tree and the Malacca cane. They fear a Spectre Huntsman and several banshees of women dead in childbed, the *Pontianak* and the *Langsuyar*, whose cry terrifies even civilised Malays. But these *sylvicolae et exsules vitae* will also start a charm with *Om* the Hindu word of power, and preface an invocation of the rice-soul with the *Basmala*. For these pagans display in their charms and songs and betrothal dialogues imagination and a bent for words and figures of speech. One would expect the artist, the Indonesian Senoi, to display this aptitude as in fact the Dayak does, but perhaps Senoi songs remain to be collected or perhaps the damage done to his speech by Mon-Annam contacts crushed it in the Senoi. But take this picture of the wild-pig by the Proto-Malay Jakun:—

> Grunt! grunt! grunt! There are the wild-pigs,
> The wild-pig's litter eating the sugar-cane,
> Eating our yams and our sweet potatoes,
> Eating all in our planted clearing.
> The wild-pig's feet are sharp and pointed.
> The wild-pig's shoulders slope and slant,
> The wild-pig's eyes are cross and squint,
> The wild-pig's bristles stiff and stubborn,
> The wild-pig's ears are pricked and pointed;
> Fat indeed the chaps of the wild-pig;
> The tail of the wild-pig's crisp and curly.

Or take this song of the sick child with its sophisticated note of regretful yearning:—

The ends of the Hibiscus burgeon,
Thicker grow the fragrant blossoms!
Give no more thought to me, granny.
Only the calyx of the fruit is left,
Only the print of my hands, granny,
Only the print of my feet,
It is only left me to sing, granny.
My heart longs for the hills, granny.
Hear the song I sing in the hut.
I will arise and go, granny. Wrap me my rice.
I will go to the forest and snare birds.
But see! My snares catch no birds, granny.
Your child is not strong enough to climb, granny,
And the basket I bear, its cords are broken.

Even the civilised Malay cannot beat that.

But who is the civilised Malay or, as he is also termed, the Deutero-Malay or Coastal Malay, of Malaya, Sumatra, Java, Bali, Lombok, Borneo, Celebes, Ternate, Tidor, Sumba and other islands? This broad-headed individual with more or less Mongoloid features, olive skin, lank black hair and thin beard is the Proto-Malay plus many foreign strains derived from intermarriage with Chinese from the Chou period onwards, with Indians from Bengal and the Deccan, with Arabs and Siamese. Differences in the mixture in different localities have produced different characteristics, so that it is possible generally to distinguish between a Bugis and a Balinese or a Minangkabau and Achinese. In Malaya there is marked difference between the tall Kelantan Malay and the smaller Malay of the southern States, partly perhaps due to better climate and the better food of a great rice area, partly perhaps to the fact that the Malays of Patani and Kelantan must have been pushed down from the continent of Asia by the Thais and not have been a mixture of aborigines and Sumatran immigrants like their southern neighbours. Many of the aborigines were Proto-Malay maritime folk. Ludovico di Varthema (1502-8) noted that if the king of Malacca wished to interfere with his people, they would threaten to "disinhabit the land, because they were men of the sea".

In the 18th century when monopoly and piracy were rife, Francis Light, the founder of Penang, could distinguish without difficulty two orders of Malay. One consisted of husbandmen who planted rice, sugar-cane and fruit trees. "The other order is employed in navigating *prows* (to all appearance not large enough for six men). For months they will skulk in bays and rivers, where there are no inhabitants, watching for the unwary traders; they spend their whole time in sloth and indolence, subsisting upon roots, wild yams and fish, and are only roused by the appearance of plunder; when they have obtained it, they return home, or to some other port to spend it. Here they are obliged to part with a share of their plunder to some chief, under whose protection they squander the remainder, and again proceed in quest of new adventure. The feudal government of the Malays encourages these pirates. Every chief is desirous of procuring many desperate fellows to bring him in plunder and execute his purposes." Even to this day the rice-planters of Kedah and Kelantan and the Minangkabau agriculturists of Negri Sembilan differ in physique and temperament from the coastal Malay whose ancestors fought d'Albuquerque, ran the gauntlet of Portuguese and Dutch patrols and pirated vessels in the Straits of Malacca.

The family of languages to which the Jakun, Dayak and Batak dialects belong is a western branch of the Malayo-Polynesian or Oceanic or Austronesian family, as it has been variously termed. This western branch includes Malay, Minangkabau, Javanese, Balinese, Bugis and the main languages of the Philippines. To an eastern branch belong the languages of Samoa, Tahiti and Tonga. Malayo-Polynesian languages are spoken from Formosa to New Zealand and from Madagascar to Easter Island. The standard pronunciation of the language of civilised Malays is that of Johor and the Riau archipelago; the same language is spoken with dialectical variations throughout Malaya, on the east coast of Sumatra and on the west coast of Borneo. It is as closely connected with Minangkabau as Sundanese with Javanese.

A connection has been surmised between this Malayo-Polynesian family of languages and an Austro-Asiatic, held to include Munda of Central India, Khassi of Assam, Mon or Talaing and Khmer or Cambodian of Indo-China, Nicobarese and Semang. The two families have been included in an Austric whole. But the discovery in Indo-China of skulls Australoid, Melanesoid, Indonesian and Negrito makes doubtful such simplification and points to the ultimate discovery of several language families.

3: BELIEFS AND RELIGION

I Primitive

To GET an impression of the beliefs and customs of the primitive Malay one has only to compare customs and beliefs still surviving in the culture of the modern Malay with those of the Khassis, as above one compared certain of their practices. Or one may again compare Malay beliefs and customs with those of the Mois of Indo-China.

Among both Malays and Khassis husbands and wives call one another not by their own names but father or mother of so-and-so, naming their child. Both break eggs for divination, and both, like the Senoi, obtain omens from dropping leaves into water. Both use a tiny reaping-knife, not to frighten the soul of the rice.

As for the Mois. Both Malays and Mois believed in the peregrination of a giant crab going in and out of his hole and so creating the rise and fall of tides. Both tell of beings with a monkey's tail and razor-edged fore-arm. Both filed and lacquered teeth at puberty and pierce the ears of girls. Betrothals for both are prefaced by a formal offering of betel. The avoidance by a husband of his mother-in-law and by a wife of her father-in-law is enjoined for both peoples. If a Moi or Malay child fall ill, its name is changed as unlucky. A child's head is shaved except for one long wisp. There are identical examples of sympathetic magic: Moi and Malay women let their hair hang loose when they are sowing so that grain may be luxuriant, and they clothe themselves lightly at harvest, so that stalks may be thin to cut. Both peoples thought that an enemy might be lamed merely by sticking a sharp bamboo in his tracks. Divination by means of an egg is practised by both peoples to discover a thief. And the ritual of a Moi sorceress exorcising sickness corresponds closely with the *séance* conducted by the Malay shaman.

As comparison with the *mana* of the Melanesians suggests a very primitive Malay idea is belief in a vital or effective force (*semangat*) "in widest commonalty spread", present in placenta, in all parts of the body, in spittle and sweat, in clippings of the hair and paring of the nails, in a person's shadow, in his name, in the water in which man or beast has washed and in the earth marked by their footprints, so that through any of these a person may be injured by sorcery. This impersonal force also vitalizes the leaves and branches of plants, stones and beads and tin and iron. In hard things like teeth and nuts, stone and iron, it is abundant beyond the ordinary. Its abundance in hair and teeth led to the sacrificing of all but one lock of a boy's hair and to the filing of teeth at puberty, the stumps left being blackened, it is supposed, to conceal the partial nature of the sacrifice. The importance of things with strong soul-substance led to bezoar stones, celts and iron being prized as fetishes. Deficiency of vital force might be remedied by diet, by rubbing with a bezoar, by the breath of the medicine-man or by a brush from his aspergillum of tough herbs. A candle-nut, a stone and an iron nail are used to fortify a child at birth and also the newly-clipped rice-baby. Two very primitive and lasting functions of the Malay medicine-man or *pawang* have been to conserve the vital spark of man and rice.

This vital force came, however, to be conceived as having personal associations and to have its character affected by its host. This personal soul departs in dreams and what it sees it dreams. A shaman's soul may enter the body of a tiger. One way for a lover to abduct the soul of a girl, which for him must be personal or else valueless, is to boil or steam any possession of hers or sand from her foot-print, reciting at the same time an incantation taught him by his later faiths, Hindu and Muslim. And religious teachers are invited by parents to spit into a child's mouth or upon his head in order to transfer to him intelligence and ability to learn to recite the Kuran. The saliva of a living saint brings great benefits to the credulous. Were not belief in the were-tiger so old, one might ascribe the very conception of a personal soul to later foreign influences, as one should probably ascribe the evolution of the idea.

Casting about for an image of the personal soul, the Malay noted the flutter of the heart, the vital spark in the fire-fly, the stridulous telegraphy of the cricket in a camphor-tree, the uncanny likeness of the stick-insect to the rattan. So he found the soul of the camphor-tree in the cicada, the soul of rice in the grass-hopper, the soul of the rattan in the stick-insect, the souls of man and the coconut-palm in a bird. In Negri Sembilan the soul of a house is said to appear as a cricket, that of a dug-out as a fire-fly. Just as a man might have a mannikin soul, so the soul of the earth was no bigger than a tray, and that of the sky no bigger than an umbrella. This was the miniature or essential universe over which the magician had control and which Malay Sufism found ready to hand.

Once a personal character was admitted for souls, it was natural for primitive man to imagine a soul returning as the ghost of an ancestor, and to ascribe malignity to the spirits of murdered men and suicides and women dying in child-birth, still-born infants, and people struck down by small-pox and cholera. Near the house where a corpse lies, no rice may be pounded and no dancing or music performed for fear of guiding the deceased back to his temporal home. And where the Malaccan habit of decent black or the fashion of wearing a white band round the hat has not been adopted, mourners put on shabby clothes and dishevel their hair, so that the dead may not recognize them. The origin of these practices has been forgotten, and they are observed now as marks of grief and respect. Notwithstanding the attitude behind such precautions, an ancestor may be kind either actively or, if he inhabits a tiger or crocodile, passively by never molesting the villagers. But the Malay woman hopes for no kindness from the girl who dying in child-birth has become a banshee in the form of a clawed bird or of a woman with a hole in her neck or with trailing viscera. And as things have souls in the form of insect or bird, so she believes a woman daring enough to keep the blood of dead child or murdered adult may command a familiar of the nigget or bottle imp type in the shape of cricket or civet-cat that will injure a rival wife or her children. There are ghost hags, that haunt kitchens and that cause nightmare. There are goblins of the soil, said to be the ghosts of men. "Spirit mediumship, metamorphosis, transmigration of souls, reincarnation are all ways in which the dead are believed to commune with the living, or to participate again in the life they have left." But probably the only dead the Muslim Malay takes seriously to-day are saints and benevolent ancestral spirits.

There are the many formless spirits of disease. And as all nature is similarly animated for the Malay, there are spirits of the river-bore, the tall cataract, the jungle-track, the forest tree. There are white spirits of the sun, black spirits of the moon and dangerous yellow spirits of the west, where the sun sets over the region of the dead. There are spirits of the beaches, the bays, the tides. Finally there are Father Sky and Mother Earth. Father Sky is no more than a name today, though for the nomadic shaman of the Far East a Sky-God was the Supreme Being whom it was his prerogative to meet in heaven, until matriarchy and agriculture exalted the Earth Goddess and finally India introduced the Hindu pantheon and substituted spirit-possession for ascension to heaven.

Trust in unseen powers and fear of them gave rise to the idea of sacrificial offerings accompanied by a ritual of prayer and invocation. Supernatural beings that inhabit Perak's state drums and trumpets might grow faint and unheeding unless drink were poured on them occasionally, as 2000 years ago blood was poured on Chinese war-drums. In the Malay offering of a pink buffalo to the spirits of district or state there survived one of the world's oldest rituals: the victim without spot, the feast in which all partake before the altar, the blood caught in a bamboo and not left to fall upon the ground, the pieces of the offering that are not set upon the altar and must be utterly consumed by those present, the celebration by night or before dawn, which no stranger may attend. At small feasts the offering is a goat, black if the sacrifice is in honour of earth-spirits, white if it is in honour of a saint or sacred animal. The commonest offering of all is a fowl. To-day the Malay has no explanation of this choice of domestic animals for the altar. But Dayak song tells why for waving and for offering no jungle-fowl, crane, argus-pheasant, kingfisher, owl or any other wild bird is worth a fowl as big as the fingers. The domestic fowl is in debt to man for rice and sugar-cane, maize and pumpkins, nest and roost and is a bird to whose redoubtable appearance familiarity has bred indifference:—

> You fowls have many crimes and many debts!
> You bear away the spirits of sickness,
> Spirits of fever and ague and headache,
> Spirits of cold, spirits of the forest. . . .
> You fowls have beaks as sharp as augers;
> Your feathers are like fringes of red thread,
> Your ear-feathers like sharpened bamboos;
> Your wings flap like folds of red cloth;
> Your tails are bent down like dragging ropes;
> Your crops weigh heavily like iron hawkbills;
> Your claws are like sharp iron knives.

In the foundations of a new house the Dayak would once place a slave-girl but now substitutes a chicken, to be crushed to death by the descent of the main house-pillar. The peninsular Malay slits the throat of fowl, goat or buffalo, sometimes bidding the vengeful children of Siva avaunt, sometimes invoking Allah. About the main house-pillar are deposited the head and feet of the offering to guard it from evil, just as Peleus cut the body of the queen of Iolcus in two and led his army between the pieces into the city. In dire illness Arabs will use swine's flesh as medicine, and if other offerings have failed to bring catches to the Kelantan fisherman, the pious depart and the forbidden pig is sacrificed on the sea-shore. In an old ceremony at Selangor fishing-stakes arrack too was offered by the Muslim celebrant to the gods of the sea.

Selangor and Negri Sembilan practise a rite traced back to ancient China and mediaeval Java as a spring festival connected with rain-making by the shedding of blood. The main feature is a mock combat, now conducted for the expulsion of malicious goblins in Malaya, Indochina and Bali. White and black goats are sacrificed. For three days or more, not exceeding seven, neither fowl nor beast may be killed nor branch broken. Then upstream a pink buffalo is slaughtered as food for the spirits, and downstream a black one for the villagers. Or flesh may be given, as in Arabia, to each villager to bury in his plot in order to placate malignant earth spirits. But the Malay learnt ways less simple for dealing with the invisible.

For an early feature in Malay magic was the shamanism that came into Malay life in central Asia along with the Mongoloid strain in his physical make-up. Commonly the same Malay word (*pawang*) is used for the ordinary medicine-man whose repertory consists of the practice of sympathetic magic, incantations, amulets and divination from leaves and candle-flame, and for the shaman who wrapt into a trance by wild music and singing learns from his familiar spirit how to cure an illness or divine a coming event.

There is from Malaya no record of elaborate initiation ceremonies for a shaman such as obtain among the Dayaks: the chanting of incantations over the neophyte to endow his fingers with the gift of diagnosis, the symbolic cleansing of his brain and eyes to give him keenness of mind and sight, the waving of fronds over him and the trampling of his body by his preceptors. A Malay shaman gets possession of a familiar spirit by inheritance from another shaman, becoming sensible of the gift in a dream or in a trance beside a grave. In Patani it is said that if a shaman neglects to bequeath his (or her) art to his heir, then his clothes, drum, censers and other stock-in-trade will generate a savage spirit. It is this ancestral helper in tiger form that is the shaman's familiar. On this familiar he (or she) may ride on night errands. By day it will guide its owner's footsteps in the forest or protect him and his cattle from material tigers and his crops from wild pigs. But besides his tiger spirit, a male shaman will command from three to a dozen or more airy nature spirits, who will descend at a *séance* to reveal the cause and cure or fatal nature of the patient's illness.

Islam tolerant of the ordinary medicine-man who lards his incantations with the Muslim confession of faith has done its best to extinguish the shaman's *séance*, and European medicine and education have collaborated, but the shaman's art is practised everywhere on rare occasions and he still commands awe and respect. In Malaya all three of the pagan races used, as we have seen, to reserve tree-burial for shamans. Malays now bury them: and many sacred (*keramat*) places are the graves of by-gone shamans. But seventy years ago in Upper Perak it was customary to place the corpse of a shaman against a tree, and still in two of the States on the west coast at least, when a shaman is in the throes of death, it is believed that the spirit of life can escape only if a hole is made in the roof, a survival of the idea of the upward flight of a shaman's soul. Tree burial must be a relic of nomadic days when ability to ascend to heaven to meet the Sky-God was the distinguishing mark of a shaman, before Mahayana Buddhism changed him into a medium for possession by spirits.

Study of the shaman throws a revealing light on one side of the Malay character. The use of such a medium is commonest where Arctic hysteria is prevalent; and there is the closest resemblance between the hysteria of the Samoyed and the *latah* of the Malay and Dayak. Both of these nervous maladies will cause sufferers to mimic the words and gestures of those who startle them. Their temporary paroxysm, like madness, the Malay attributes to possession by a spirit. But ascent to heaven to consult the Sky-God was the distinguishing prerogative of a shaman till India changed him into a vehicle for possession by spirits.

All the characteristics of the shaman have been found by modern science in patients suffering from hysterical delirium. In the hysterical, excitement provokes an outbreak. Their visual hallucinations are especially visions of animals and of fantastic processions, in which dead persons, devils and ghosts swarm. The patient will become cataleptic and in somnambulistic dialogue copy the peculiarities of dead relatives and acquaintances, changing the voice for each. Sometimes he or she uses a pseudo-language, arranging meaningless words and sounds from several tongues. One of Jung's patients declared that she lost her body and went to distant places whither spirits led her. Once she was hysterically blind for half an hour, did not see the candle on the table and had to be led. She so influenced her relatives that three of her brothers and sisters also began to have hallucinations. Another woman had to have a splinter cut out of her finger. "Without any kind of bodily change, she suddenly saw herself sitting beside a brook in a beautiful meadow, plucking flowers." Another gradually lost her abnormal sensitiveness and six months later was caught cheating at a *séance*, concealing small objects in her dress and throwing them up in the air, wanting to restore the lost belief in her supernatural powers. Jung's diagnosis of hysteria might have been made from a study of the Malay shaman alone.

To evoke the condition of automatism needed for a *séance* the Malay shaman employs well-recognized methods. Incense is burnt beside him. The thud of his attendant's drum waxes ever louder and more frantic. Holding a grass brush with stiff extended arm, he stares fixedly at a candle, quivers, begins to grow rigid and swoons as each spirit takes possession of him. Although the pious Muslim Malay dismisses these trances as make-believe, they prepared the way for the visions of the Malay Sufi mystic. And their widespread existence is evidence of a hysterical streak in the Malay that has been a motive power in Indonesian politics.

II Hinduism

Lately evidence has accumulated to indicate early Indian visits to Malaya. Probably it was an Indian ship that brought an Attic vase of the 5th century B.C. to Perlis. Roman beads from Kota Tinggi in Johor were left, it is inferred, by Indian traders at the beginning of the Christian era. Inscriptions are testimony to the presence of Hinayana and Mahayana Buddhists in Kedah in the 4th century. To the next century belong a bronze Hinayana Buddha in the Greek style of Amaravati found in Kedah and two Hinayana Buddhist images of Gupta style from the Kinta valley in Perak. Then Pallavas from the Coromandel coast founded Hindu settlements in Kedah, on what is now called the Bujang river but what was probably once the Bujangga or Dragon river, building little temples from whose ruins have been dug an image of Ganesha, a bronze Siva trident, and the roof of a miniature bronze shrine with cross-legged Rishis at each corner betokening the Sivaite cult. The 8th century saw northern Malaya under the influence of Indian Buddhists again, this time Mahayanists from the Pala kingdom of Bengal. A bronze casket from the foundation deposits of a Kedah temple contained miniature weapons of Ajanta type, that later appear in carvings on Bara-Budur. One of them was in the form of a broad spatulate dagger associated in Java with Siva in his Tantric form of a demon Bhairawa, and famous throughout the Malay world from a specimen (*churika Mandakini*) in the Minangkabau regalia. Tantric doctrine connected Sivaism and Buddhism. And to the same period as the Kedah casket belong two many-armed (and therefore Mahayana) Avalokitesvaras from Perak, one from Bidor and one from Sungai Siput. As far down as Perak Malaya became part of the great Malay Buddhist kingdom of Sri Vijaya, under the Sailendras or Indras of the Mountain, one of whom built Bara-Budur, the most famous monument in Java. It is hardly probable that the Chula raids of the 11th century affected the beliefs of the Malay. But Kedah, Patani and Kelantan were greatly affected by the culture of Hindu Majapahit, which conquered Sri Vijaya and her colonies between 1338 and 1365. In Kedah linguistic traces remain, and in Kelantan the shadow-play and many of the ceremonies still exhibit Javanese Hindu characteristics. A rite (*main Putri*) for ' cleansing ' Kelantan, where a magician, male or female, takes the part of Siva's Sakti, is a survival of a Tantric orgy where union with the divine was effected through a nude woman worshipped as a goddess. It recalls the human sacrifices to a spirit called P'o-to-li in Cambodia before 589 A.D. and in Trengganu in 1349 to Kali or Siva's consort as the Hindu goddess of death. Although a Trengganu stele proves that Islam had reached that country in the 14th century, yet until Malacca was converted early in the next, the religion of nearly all the peninsular Malays was a mixture of Hinduism and Buddhism for the educated and animism and shamanism for the peasant.

More than a millenium of Buddhist and Hindu influences have left comparatively few material relics. The "Kedah Annals" record how on conversion to Islam the Malays destroyed all the idols they were accustomed to worship, together with the idols handed down from their ancestors. In the first half of the 17th century Hamzah the mystical poet from Barus adjured the Sumatran Malays

> Burn the sheath and draw the sword!
> Be idols abandoned and Allah obeyed![1]

And the work of destruction was thorough.

On the spiritual side Sanskrit words for "religion", "fasting", "teacher", "heaven" and "hell" had become too familiar to be abandoned. A lot of Hindu ritual also remained, though hard to extract from Muslim practices brought by Indian missionaries whose ancestors had been Hindus. There are, for example, twelve purificatory rites to cleanse a Brahmin from original sin. Between these (of which several may be performed together) and the main

[1] See Appendix A, p. 182.

incidents of a Malay child's life there is such close coincidence that, however they came to the Malay, those incidents are clearly survivals of Hinduism, corroborated by the many Sanskrit words employed in the Malay ceremonies. The twelve Hindu rites are as follows:—

(1) There is a ritual of consummation spoken on the fourth or fifth day of marriage ceremonies, with which the ceremonial bathing of the couple, seated on a rice-mortar, on or before the seventh day of a Malay wedding may have been associated.

(2) Marriage generally in Malaya is full of such Hindu ritual as the sitting in state of the couple dressed as Rajas for the day and required to feed one another with rice in front of their neighbours. Hindu, too, is the sending of creese or head-dress by a Malay Raja to represent his person at a marriage with a wife of humble origin.

(3) and (4) Two ceremonies are performed together in the seventh month of pregnancy, the first to ensure the birth of a son and the second the parting of the hair of the prospective mother. These correspond to a Malay ceremony termed *melenggang perut*.

(5) An infant's tongue is touched thrice at birth with honey and *ghi*, a verse from the Rig-Veda being recited to wish the child long life and happiness. This rite is observed by Arab, Indian and Malay Muslims, with the omission, of course, of the verse from the Rig-Veda.

(6) A name is whispered into the child's ear by the parents on the tenth or twelfth day.

(7) In the fourth month the Brahmin child is taken out to see the sun. In Malaya, before being laid in a swinging cot for the first time, children are introduced to mother earth and to father water, personifications known to the Hindu.

BELIEFS AND RELIGION

(8) The Brahmin child is fed with rice about the sixth month, a ceremony for which there appears to be no Malay equivalent.

(9) In the third year a boy's head is shaved except for one lock, Brahmin and Malay both clipping it with seven strokes of the scissors.

(10) A Brahmin boy is invested with the sacred cord and is the object of elaborate ritual, when he is delivered to his *guru* or religious teacher. The Muslim Malay is handed over to his Kuran teacher with considerable ceremony.

(11) At puberty the lock on the Brahmin boy's head is cut off. This is done by Malays with great ceremony before circumcision, which precedes puberty.

(12) Brahmins and Indian and Malay Muslims hold a feast on a youth's return home after the completion of his religious studies.

The great sacrifices held periodically before the British period to cleanse (*palis; pelas* Perak) Perak and Kelantan of evil spirits and appease guardian spirits, resemble similar sacrifices in Majapahit and combine ancestor worship and shamanism with Hindu and Muslim elements. The State shaman conducted them.

As Hindus the Malays of mediaeval Malacca burnt their dead. But if ever the wives and concubines of Malay rajas and chiefs performed suttee like widows in Java and Bali, no trace of the custom remains except a chance remark of Ludovico di Varthema that in Sumatra (1502–8) women were burnt alive.

The two most elaborate Hindu rituals to survive are the enthronement ceremony of a Malay king (pp. 65–9), and the ceremony preluding dramatic shows, such as the sacrifice and invocation before episodes from the Ramayana are enacted on the screen of the shadow-play at some harvest, marriage or circumcision festival. Wearing the yellow scarf appropriate to gods and kings about his shoulders, the Kelantan reciter or master of the play claims to be the incarnation or representative of Vishnu. Cross-legged he sits before a tray of offerings for the spirits of the four quarters of the world, spirits of ocean and forest, Ganesha, Arjuna, Sang Bima and the Bhutas. There is a special plate of uncooked rice, and there are a raw egg, raw thread and money for Batara Guru, that is, Siva the supreme teacher and, as Nataraja, lord of dancers and king of actors. His body fumigated with the smoke of incense, the master of the play calls indiscriminately upon Siva, Ganesha, and the demigods of the Ramayana and Mahabharata to partake of the offerings. Then censing the leather puppets that represent Siva and Vishnu, he begs them to drive away all spirits of evil. At the end of the performance he bids a formal farewell to his ghostly troupe: "Om! I salute you. Gentle rain is falling to refresh the nymphs of Siva's heaven after the heat. Dust is flying up into the air, a sign that by virtue of our devotions the gods are mounting to Suralaya, their heaven. Open the big gates! For Siva the destroyer is descending from the summit of heaven to expel all evil powers, all spirits of disease. Before earth was of the size of a foot or the vault of heaven was framed, when only the throne of Allah and the tablet of fate and the Kuran existed, I was the original magician, uttering the original incantation to disperse spirits of evil. It bid them disperse to their masters, King Solomon, Siva, the Spectre Huntsman, Vishnu and the great Dragon at the navel of the sea. It is not I who bid them go but the original primal salutation that bids them; not I but Siva the first of actors, not I but Siva, the first of teachers. And my magic has the power of that teacher's magic. One! Three! Five! Seven! Avaunt! Avaunt."

For Hindu magic, as well as Hindu prayer and sacrifice, was once familiar to the Malay. India gave him his greatest fetish in a ruler who was an incarnation of Indra or Vishnu or other deity, whose body affected the weather and who made his kingdom into an image of the heavenly world of stars and gods. And this type of ruler was not one to neglect magic. A 9th century inscription in Champa records the appointment in Java of a royal official with a Sanskrit title, *siddhayatra*, to study the subject. Certainly the Malay medicine-man and shaman were alert to learn all the secrets they could from Hinduism, as later they were quick to borrow from Sufi mysticism; although nowadays it is only the Malay magician of remote hamlets who (Muslim though he is) yet calls on Siva by his many titles, Mahadeva or Great Lord, Kala destroyer of life, Spectre Huntsman or Rudra the storm-god, leader of lost souls. If a person is sick, it is Siva whom this magician entreats to call off his followers from plaguing the patient, and should recovery ensue, it is to Siva that thank-offerings are presented. When soil is violated by the planting of rice or house-pillars, it is Siva who is invoked to restrain malicious gnomes and goblins. If a hunter kills a deer, it is Siva who can avert the malice of the dead body. To recover lost property, the Malay may still make offerings to Siva, who, he will tell you, though still a Raja, is now one of Islam's infidel djinns.

The wife of Siva was known to the Malay as Mahadewi, Great Goddess, or Kumari, the Damsel. Sri for him was the goddess of rice-fields, who ousted Mother Earth as Siva ousted Father Sky. Brahma hardly enters into Malay magic. In Kelantan Krishna is invoked to cure snake-bites and stings. Rahu who causes eclipse of sun and moon, Danu who inhabits the rainbow, Bhutas and Raksasas are now, like the Hindu gods, regarded as infidel djinns.

Most of such adaptations of the old faith to the new must have been due, as has been said, to early Muslim missionaries from India, who brought with them a syncretism of Hindu and Muslim beliefs and practices. It must have been some Indian who adapted for the Malay a charm from the Atharva-Veda to arouse the passionate love of a woman:—

In the name of Allah, the Merciful, the Compassionate!
Burn, burn, sand and earth!
I burn the heart of my beloved
And my fire is the arrow of Arjuna.
If I burnt a mountain, it would fall;
If I burnt rock, it would be riven.
I am burning the heart of my beloved,
So that she is broken and hot with love,
That giveth her no rest night or day,
Burning ever as this sand burns.
Let her cease to love parents and friends!
If she sleeps, awaken her!
If she awakes, cause her to rise and come,
Yielding herself unto me,
Devoid of shame and discretion!
By virtue of the poison of Arjuna's arrow,
By virtue of the invocation "There is no God but Allah and Muhammad is His Prophet."[1]

The incantation in the Atharva-Veda is practically identical. But the Hindu lover pierced the heart of a clay effigy by means of a bow with a hempen string carrying the terrible arrow of Kama, Hindu god of love, barbed with a thorn and plumed with an owl feather. The Malay talked of Arjuna's arrow, and fried earth from the girl's footprint or the print of her carriage-wheels along with jasmine buds. In late Hebrew charms the sorcerer cries: "Ye holy powerful angels! just as this pot is burnt in the fire, so shall ye burn in the heart of so-and-so to follow after this girl." It is easy, therefore, to exaggerate the influence of genuine Hindu magic on the Malay. Largely his indebtedness to India has been for Assyrio-Babylonian charms infected with Hindu mythology. In Semitic magic as in Hindu the exorcist must know a word of power, the name or description of the demons he would expel, and something material, be it any amulet or wax figure, to aid his muttered incantation.

[1] See Appendix A, p. 182.

In Semitic magic, as in Malay, the exorcist goes through a catalogue of ghosts and demons, not to miss any cause for his patient's illness, and he disclaims power for himself and ascribes his knowledge to some "lord of incantation".

The most impressive lesson taught the Malay by Hinduism was that the seer is born of austerity, and that fasting and abstinence win magic and victory in love and war. Tomé Pires tells how in his time (1512) there were 50,000 ascetics (*orang bertapa*) in Java, belonging to three or four orders. None of them knew woman and some neither ate rice nor drank wine. The Moors (or Muslims) respected them and gave them alms. These ascetics practising Hindu austerities must have existed at all Hinduized centres in the Malay world. For it was the aim of the Malay's Hindu teacher, as afterwards of his Sufi teacher, to guide his pupils to pass from ritual to that inner knowledge which was believed to give supernatural power, and it is this side of his Hindu borrowings that has left a lasting impression on the Malay mind, an impression far more important than the survival of an outworn shibboleth on the lips of illiterate village medicine-men.

III Islam

In Indonesia more than 85 per cent. of the population now profess the religion of Muhammad, and in Malaya all the Malays have been Muslims for several centuries.

Marco Polo in 1292 found Islam established by "Saracen" traders at Perlak, a little port on the north coast of Sumatra. Neighbouring districts like Samudra and Pasai also accepted this new faith imported by Indians, whose cosmopolitan novelty, apparent affluence and pharmacopoea of herbs and amulets had for the Indonesian the attraction that escapist tales of travel, spiritualism and science have had for Europe in recent times. A daughter of the ruler of Perlak married the first Muslim Sultan of Pasai, Malik al-Salih who died in 1297. And by the middle of the 14th century Islam had reached the north of Malaya, as is proved by the Trengganu stele with the first known Perso-Arabic script in the Malay world.

How Islam came to Malacca, whence it spread to Java and Borneo and Celebes, is set forth in the *Suma Oriental* of Tomé Pires, a Portuguese accountant, who wrote his book in Malacca and India in 1512–1515. From this, the earliest Portuguese account, it appears that in the time of Megat Iskandar Shah, the first ruler of Malacca, Javanese trade was largely diverted there from Pasai. "And some rich Moorish merchants moved from Pasai to Malacca, Parsis as well as Bengalis and Arabian Moors, for at that time there were a large number of merchants belonging to these three nations, and they were very rich, with large businesses and fortunes . . . and they brought with them mollahs and priests learned in the sect of Muhammad . . . Iskandar Shah was pleased with the said Moorish merchants and did them honour, giving them places to live in and a place for their mosques. . . . Trade began to grow greatly—chiefly because the said Moors were rich—and Iskandar Shah derived great profit and satisfaction from it and gave them jurisdiction over themselves. . . . And there were many Moors and many mollahs who were trying hard to make the king turn Moor, and the king of Pasai greatly desired it. The said king Iskandar Shah did in fact come to want to establish the said priests and to like them. When this news came, the king of Pasai on the advice of the priests he had sent there, secretly sent others of greater authority to impose upon him and turn him away from his race and heathenry and to convert him, and this by underhand means and not publicly. . . . At last when he was seventy-two years old, the said King Iskandar Shah turned Moor, with all his house and married the king of Pasai's daughter. And not only did he himself turn Moor, but also in the course of time he made all his people do the same." Within half a century Malacca became a centre of Islamic studies, converted Pahang and the south of Malaya by force of arms, saw Kedah embrace Islam, subdued Kampar and Indragiri and Siak in Sumatra and made their rulers accept the new faith, and despatched missionaries to Java and down to the Malay archipelago along every trade-route.

On their first voyage home from the Indies the Dutch took back a Javanese religious treatise, probably compiled by a Javanese student at Malacca and citing among its authorities the *Hadith*, Ghazali's *Ihya 'ulum al-din*, Nawawi's *Talkhis al-minhaj* and Abu-Shukur's *Tamhid*. For Malay students of Islam would wander far in search of knowledge. The famous Malay mystic Hamzah, of Barus in Sumatra, whose works were burnt as heretical, not only visited Mecca and Medinah but travelled in quest of truth to Ayuthia in Siam, to Bantan and Kudus in Java and to Pahang. A MS. in the Marsden collection gives one of the well-known lists of teachers who from generation to generation had transmitted the Sufi doctrines of the Shattariah order "that came from the Messenger of Allah whom Allah bless and preserve, from the lord 'Ali son of Abi Talib, with whom may Allah be well pleased, who taught the lord Husain the Martyr, who taught the lord Zain al-'abidin, who taught Imam Muhammad al-Baqir, who taught the blessed Imam Ja'afar al-Sadik" (d. A.D. 886) and so on down to the famous 'Abd al-Rauf (ca. 1661), son of 'Ali, of the same race as Hamzah of Barus and a man of Singkel, who taught Shaikh Haji 'Abd al-muhyi of the village Saparwadi in Karang (Preanger, Java), who taught Pakir Kiai Agus Nazim al-din of the same place, who taught Kiai Haji Muhammad Yunus of the same place, who taught Kiai Mas, Penghulu of Bandong, who taught Haji 'Abdullah bin 'Abd al-Malik who lived at Pulau Rusa in Trengganu, who taught Lebai Bidin son of Ahmat, an Achinese."

The early missionaries of Islam found Hinduized courts, officials administering a system of Hindu and customary law, medicine-men looking to shaman *séance* and Hindu magic and astrology for the cure of disease and for their clients' success in love and war. "Both the men and women of Malacca," writes Tomé Pires, "are fond of mimes after the fashion of Java," revelling in the shadow-play with its repertories from those favourite Hindu epics, the Mahabharata and Ramayana. This was the society which the missionaries from India changed by every method of propaganda at their command. Hindu incantations were now called prayers (*do'a* Ar.) and made unobjectionable by the addition of the new confession of faith, acknowledging the One God and Muhammad His latest Prophet:—

It is not I who get rid of the evils of black magic,
It is Batara Guru; it is the gods of the Hindu heaven,
It is seven deities of supernatural power.
Son of Batara Kala, grandson of Ganesa!
Descend and dispel all hazard and ill-luck,
Dispel them from the home of all the sons of Adam!
The sword of Vishnu is before my face.
Genies in whose keeping are earth and water,
Genies in whose lap is the world,
Return ye to your place, the broken rock at the navel of the seas!
Enter not the line drawn by my teacher!
If ye enter, I will curse you with the words of the Prophet Solomon;
I will curse you with the creed, "There is no God but Allah and Muhammad is His Prophet."[1]

The Perak medicine-man was taught to invoke his predecessors of old and Siva and Vishnu to defend the fellers of a new rice clearing from the malice of Arabian genies, Persian fairies, Hindu demigods and Indonesian nature spirits and to ascribe his incantation to Siva the Divine Teacher, Siva the Destroyer, Brahma and Luqman al-Hakim, father of Arabian magic. The syncretism was crude but effective. Equally effective was the supplanting of the heroes of the Hindu epics, Sri Rama, Laksamana, Arjuna, by a fictitious picture of Alexander the Great as a forerunner of Muhammad in the fight for monotheism; and Malay rulers, who had been incarnations of Indra and Vishnu, were content to be made descendants of a Macedon-

[1] See Appendix A, p. 182-3.

ian man-god through the Sassanian kings of Persia. In place of the shaman's fearful initiation in the forest and of the fasting and seclusion copied from Hindu ascetics in order to acquire magic, the Malay now submitted to listen shrouded to the prayers for the dead read over him; fasting, he would repeat the name of Allah five thousand times, until hysteria brought hideous visions of ravening tiger or coiling snake to be succeeded in those who endured by visions of prophets and angels teaching the neophyte the magic arts for which he craved.

For though the Malay is an orthodox Sunni of the school of Shafi'i, there were Shia' elements in the form of Muhammadanism he learnt originally from India. These elements were a crude pantheism, a Gnostic concern with mystic names and formulae and the worship of innumerable saints. The reverence for saints permitted offerings at the graves of ancestors, founders of settlements, rulers, religious teachers and even before rocks and trees. Immediately after his enthronement, for example, a Sultan of Perak is supposed to pay a pilgrimage to the graves of former rulers. As for mystic names and formulae, in Hindu days the Malay had invoked nature-spirits and deities by every possible designation so that an incantation might not go astray. It was therefore no break with tradition to invoke Allah by all His Excellent Names and to replace *Om* the Hindu word of power with the Arabic *Kun* "Let it be" and with the *Basmala*, whose recital can attract fish from all the seas, make the barren fruitful, lay the tyrant low and bring honour and salvation. The Malay's new teachers taught him how the appropriate Arab text written on an amulet at the right astrological moment in scented rosewater musk and saffron with a recitation of the proper formula would save a woman from all attempts on her virtue even by the black art and would protect a man from bullet, spear, pestilence and shipwreck. The hexagonal seal of Solomon attracted the interest once bestowed on the Laksamana line, which Sita in the Ramayana crossed to her undoing.

As for mysticism even the court of mediaeval Malacca was so interested that on two occasions envoys were sent to Pasai to propound hard problems for solution. Sultan Mansur Shah sent an offering of gold and two slave-girls to any one in Pasai who could tell if those in heaven and those in hell abide in their respective places forever. Later Sultan Mahmud sent two cockatoos and a knife inlaid with gold for any Pasai theologian who could solve the paradox that whoever believed God had created and bestowed His gifts from all eternity was an infidel and whoever disbelieved it was an infidel. The answer to the first problem Malays found in the popular *Insan al-Kamil* or Perfect Man of al-Jili, who held that the sufferers' power of endurance being a divine gift extinguished the fire or else that their torment was changed to pleasure. To the second question the Malay knew two answers, the orthodox one that spirit (*ruh*) is not eternal but created, and the unorthodox one that the word of creation merely raised what was already existent though not manifest.

In its chances and changes the Muhammadanism of the Malays has followed the movements of the Muslim world. There has been the recurrent conflict between the transcendentalism of orthodox theologians, for whom God is in heaven, and popular mysticism, which starting from animism inclines towards a pantheism that finds Him closer than the veins of one's neck.

Malacca in the 16th century and Acheh in the first half of the 17th saw the same compromise and harmony between orthodoxy and Sufism that then characterized Islam in the Near East, a compromise of which the Malays owing their new religion to India were hardly conscious. As the centre of Malay commerce after the Portuguese capture of Malacca in 1511, Acheh attracted to its capital men of profound learning of the mediaeval type, missionaries of Islam from India, Arabia and even Egypt. While the orthodox preached the necessity of ritual and doctrine for man's communion with his Maker, the exponents of a Sufism derived from

India and from 17th century Medinah disallowed any distinction between God and man, denied that there was any receiver or offerer of prayer and declared that one who offers prayer is not a monotheist. Two of Acheh's foremost heterodox mystics were Sumatran Malays, Hamzah of Barus (c. 1600) and Shams al-din of Pasai (d. 1630), and their mystic doctrines became known throughout the Malay world. For the orthodox Allah is omniscient but for Hamzah He is identical with man and the universe. Sole and absolute He contains all being and all worlds, subject and object, lover and beloved, heat and cold, good and evil, the Ka'abah and the heathen temple. Following ibn 'Arabi, Hamzah accepts Allah or Being as not only sole but bound by necessity, so that it is not the arbitrary will of God but the necessity of His Being that makes one man a Muslim and another not. God is a sea, immobile, without ripple but with potential waves, that stirred by his creative word have come to represent this world of appearance but always have the reality of the sea. Absolute Being is identical with the spiritual essence of man, wherefore it is said in the Kuran, "Wheresoever you turn, there is the face of God". For the mystic who attains wisdom or gnosis (*ma'rifat*), the veil between lover and beloved falls away.

Shams al-din also employs the image of sea and waves and surge. Man's Being for him is God's Being, the individuality of man being no more than a name. Man's outward body is no more than a wave and life no more than surge in God's infinite sea. For Shams al-din all but God is the reflection on a screen by the hand that moves the puppets. The outstanding features of his speculations are the doctrines of the Unity of Existence and of the Perfect Man, the mirror by which God is revealed to Himself and therefore the final cause of creation. "In more than one respect his system stands midway between Indian and Javanese forms of Islamic mysticism."

Then in 1637 there arrived in Acheh from Rajputana a famous interpreter of Ghazali's orthodox mysticism, one

Nur al-din ibn 'Ali from Ranir in Bikanir, the author of the *Bustan al-Salatin* and other works, who compared himself with a cup-bearer circulating the wine of the Prophet. For him there was no doubt about the answer to the second question Sultan Mansur Shah had put to the theologians of Pasai. Spirit for him was not eternal but created, and he condemned the pantheistic identification of man and the world with God. The heretical works of the two Sumatian mystics he got burned. Fortunately some of them escaped the fire. For the skill with which these Malays with a vocabulary lacking in abstract terms were able to grasp and introduce Sufi mysticism to their world is very remarkable, and though their ideas were not original, in no other field has the Malay mind ever displayed such intellectual ability and subtlety. For Shams al-din Islamic theology meant metaphysical speculation in which the importance of intellectual processes is stressed above that of emotion. But the ordinary Malay, untrained to distinguish between orthodox and heterodox, was content to seek a vent for spiritual emotion in mystic reverie induced by Yogi postures, by closing the eyes and noting the breath in the nostrils, by the interminable counting of rosaries or the repeated chanting of his profession of faith. Metaphysics were above his head, and his proofs of the identity of God and man were based on such crude evidence as the quaternity of the first Caliphs, the Archangels, the founders of the schools of Islamic law, and the letters that in Arabic spell the name of Muhammad and the word Allah. Man he conceived to be a microcosm, whose backbone corresponded to the pillar of God's throne, his bile to fire, his phlegm to water, his belly to the ocean, his spirit to a bird. To the mystic union of the lover and the beloved he attached a literal and carnal meaning, and his medicine-man, who had already grafted Hindu beliefs on to primitive animism, welcomed a new weapon for his spiritual armoury, giving to the love-charm called since Hindu times the arrow of Arjuna the new name of the Arrow of Gnosis, that made lover and beloved one.

In the name of God, the Merciful, the Compassionate!
I boil and steam this sand from my beloved's foot-print

To be a dart made powerful by Allah,
Whose will I am bringing to pass;
I take this sand through my knowledge (*ma'rifat*) of Allah.
If I shoot at a mountain, it falls;
If I shoot at rock, the rock is riven,[1]

and so and so on, as in the Hindu charm already quoted above. To guard his life during sleep the Kelantan peasant draws a deep breath and recites:—

I am the real Muhammad!
It is not I who speak, Muhammad is speaking.
First spirit was created, then the body.
This evening is as the womb of my mother;
Only if it is destroyed, can I be destroyed!
My being is Thy being,
My being is one with Thy being!
I retreat into the enclosure,
"There is no God but God! Huwa,"
The womb of my mother, the Light of Muhammad,
Until daybreak to-morrow.[2]

Only if Allah and Muhammad are parted, can I and my beloved be parted! Only if Allah and Muhammad suffer harm, can I suffer harm! These are frequent vaunts in Malay adjurations. As I have written elsewhere, "One is reminded of the Hermetic discourse known by the name of Poimandres, wherein the initiated claims complete knowledge of the name and nature of God and complete equality with Him and addresses Him—'if anything happen to me in this year, this month, this day or this hour, it will happen to the great God also'." A Persian heretic, Mansur Hallaj, would say to one man, "Thou art Noah", to another, "Thou art Moses", to a third, "Thou art Muhammad". And the same crude mysticism inspired the Malay magician, who, when planting the main post of his fishing-stakes, would cry that it was resting against the pillar of God's throne, that Allah was handing it down and Muhammad receiving it. An old Perak charm-book advises the lover that over a posy

[1] See Appendix A, p. 183.
[2] See Appendix A, p. 183.

of flowers for his mistress he should recite, "*I* am Allah, the Divine Reality, Who blesseth all the worlds". Hardly more covert is the threat of a Kelantan exorcist to malignant genies that the organs of the patient they are afflicting are the habitations of the four Archangels and the first four Caliphs and that on the patient's feet move Allah and His Prophet. In the Bhagavad-Gita it is written of the Eternal Spirit "everywhere are Its hands and feet", and many of the Indian missionaries of Islam failed to rise above a literal interpretation of metaphysical mysteries. It is not, therefore, surprising that the extrovert mind of their disciple, the Malay medicine-man, borrowed the crudest of pantheist ideas to fortify and comfort his patients in their hour of need.

Malay theologians, however, at the end of the 18th century followed as usual the fashion of the Near East, which then turned back to the orthodox mysticism of al-Ghazali. 'Abd al-Samad of Palembang spent ten years (1779–1789) translating his famous work "The revival of religion" (*Ihya Ulum al-din*) into Malay, and Daud ibn 'Abdillah ibn Idris of Patani also translated it along with al-Ghazali's "Book of Secrets" (*Kitab al-asrar*) and his "Book of approach to God" (*Kitab al-kurbat ila Allah*), his work being published at Mecca in 1824.

But already about the middle of the 18th century the Near East had experienced the Wahhabi reformation with its hatred of animism (and the Muslim counterpart, pantheism) and its condemnation of all pagan survivals in Muslim culture and of the idolatrous worship of saints. Fifty years later it reached India and a century ago led in Sumatra to the white-clad Padri rising in protest against heathen notions of relationship and inheritance that are still cherished under the Minangkabau matriarchy. The Wahhabi movement, allied with political ends, was behind the idea of Pan-Islamism. But that notion of a far-flung Muslim theocracy, though taken up by the Sublime Porte to enhance its political prestige, made little or no appeal to Malays, whose loyalties were still parochial. Nor had it a long life.

For one of the consequences of the first world-war was the extinction of the Turkish Caliphate.

Another was the seizure of Mecca by a Wahhabi king. The triumph of this fundamentalist diminished the status and comfort of Indonesian Shafi'is in the Holy City and diverted more Malay theological students to the al-Azhar university at Cairo. There Muhammad 'Abduh (d. 1905) had preached a modernism already popular in some Malay circles for its puritan ideal of religion freed from superstition and its advocacy of a scientific education for the transformation of djinns into microbes. But having no translations of European works on logic and philosophy, these modernists saw nothing wrong in brushing aside historical evidence in order to exalt their Prophet. And a new cult of Muhammad not only became a convenient counterblast to the Christian exaltation of Christ but brought the Malay back to the Perfect Man and Sufism. In Malaya, however, as elsewhere the orthodox Muslim authorities remained so rigidly conservative that 1934 saw the burning of a tract on free will because it had been compiled at the instance of a Malay modernist from the Egyptian university. Even now Malay orthodoxy dislikes the acceptance of interest from banks, companies and co-operative societies. And in fact, Malay modernism has owed far less to conservative al-Azhar than to the secular education imparted by Dutch and English to lay pupils whose ignorance of theology has compelled them to air their advanced views only by such external signs as the adoption of European clothes, the use of the Roman alphabet and the exaltation of a vernacular they know above Arabic of which they have no knowledge. Generally, however, Malaya lagged well behind Java in adopting these changes. For a while the Malays dallied with the Ahmedia movement, started in the Panjab in 1900 by Mirza Ghulam Ahmed Kadiani, who in spite of a modernist outlook held that Christ did not die on the Cross but migrated and is buried at Srinagar in Kashmir, and who himself claimed to be a Mahdi, the incarnation of Jesus and Muhammad. Later the Malay became interested in the Muhammadiah party of Netherlands India, modernists who are feared and distrusted by the traditionalists or Islamiah party. The Muhammadiah party would interpret the Kuran in the light of modern knowledge and aim at the physical and intellectual advancement of the race. With such an ideal the Sufi is hardly in accord. So in a bid to command popular support, these modernists took the word *tasawwuf* the "mysticism" of the Sufi with its age-long appeal to Indonesian mentality and applied it to a system of ethics bearing on practical life. Needless to say, this system in the eyes of traditionalists is not Sufi mysticism at all, however great its pragmatical value.

Throughout the Muslim world the second world war had startling repercussions. Even before it, the Islamic theory of the brotherhood of all believers had been reinforced by the spread of democratic ideas, and the war was to discover the prestige of Malay royalty so undermined that in Sumatra Sultans were murdered in defiance of the immemorial sanctity of an anointed king. Never before the war did one meet a peninsular Malay who would profess neutrality towards all religions or was inclined to extol his Hindu past as a golden age of freedom and self-government. Never before the war could one imagine a Malay woman speaking from a public platform or sitting in a legislative council. After it nationalist aspirations extinguished or at any rate silenced objections to female education; and the Malay woman, who never tolerated purdah, entered the political arena.

4: SOCIAL SYSTEMS

I Patriarchal

IN THE Malay peninsula the Negrito has no tribal organization, but lives in family groups with male heads and equality among all the members. The Indonesian Senoi lives in similar groups with male heads, each group having joint ownership of clearings, fruits, trees, forests and streams, though individuals may acquire private property by bartering rattans or a blow-pipe. On marriage, a Senoi couple may join either of the partners' families, and if the wife has no brother or brother's son of competent age, her husband may even become head of her family. The social system of the Jakun shows features that may be primitive or borrowed from civilized neighbours, especially the Minangkabaus.

The civilised Malays of the peninsula have lived for centuries under Rajas with a Hindu tradition, whose descent and titles even in matrilineal Negri Sembilan go from father to son. Hindu influence is illustrated by the survival in Malay tradition and literature of the various Hindu forms of marriage. There was capture or forcible abduction appropriate to Kshatriyas, and by Malays termed *panjat angkara*. The "Malay Annals" give an example in the abduction and marriage of a daughter of Sri Nara 'diraja in old Malacca by a Javanese Patih Adam, who entered her house by force, tied her to himself and declared that if he was to be killed he would first kill the girl. Of the second form of Hindu marriage or peaceful abduction (*panjat 'adat*) through a maid or go-between Malay romance has many examples. The "Malay Annals" give the case of Hang Nadim sailing to Pahang and bribing a duenna to carry off the affianced daughter of the Pahang Bendahara as a bride for Mahmud, last Sultan of Malacca. The third form of Hindu marriage, *svayamivara* or *silambari* as Malays corrupted it, was known to them from their version of the

Ramayana, and figures only in their romance, the bride choosing from among rival suitors after a contest of wit or arms. The love-marriage without the consent of parents occurs very seldom and sometimes leads to prosecution under the Indian Penal Code. The most usual form of Hindu marriage, the purchase of a girl from her parents, took the place in the Malay world of a more primitive exchange of presents between the families of bride and groom. A relic of Hindu practice is the prejudice against a younger daughter being married before an elder. And the part of the wedding that Malays still regard as of the greatest ceremonial importance is the Hindu sitting in state of bride and groom dressed as prince and princess for the day, while they feed one another with gobbets of rice before all their neighbours.

But at the beginning of the 15th century, Malacca, followed gradually by the rest of the peninsula, embraced Islam and adopted the Muhammadan marriage law. The change was gradual. Tomé Pires, writing of Malacca in 1512, say, "heathens marry with Moorish women and a Moor with a heathen woman with their proper ceremonies". By Muhammadan law a Malay may marry not more than four women at once, though few but Rajas and wealthy men availed themselves of this latitude and nowadays monogamy is the common practice. As a Muslim, a Malay may marry only a Muslim, Christian or Jewess, but not a pagan. He observes the Muslim degrees of affinity, except in Negri Sembilan where Minangkabau custom forbids the marriage not only of the descendants of a common ancestress but even of brothers' children. As a Muslim the Malay may marry the sister or near relative of a deceased or divorced wife, but not two near relatives at the same time. Under Shafi'ite law a marriage may be declared null if either party is a leper, a lunatic, scrofulous or unable to consummate it. Marriage is a contract legalized by a *kadli*, or, in his absence, by anyone acquainted with Muslim law, before witnesses, and must be accepted by both husband and wife in person or through proper representatives. A Malay bride's guardian or *wali* commonly employs an agent versed in the ritual. That guardian must be an ascending agnate, father or grandfather, never an uncle or brother. If there is no *wali* or a *wali* refuse to let his ward get married, the *kadli* can appoint a guardian. If the bride is a minor, then following the school of Hanafiah instead of that of Shafi'i, the Malays permit her to repudiate the marriage contract when she becomes adult. As for dowry, which unlike the Hindu bride-price paid to parents[1] is a gift to the bride (*mahr* Ar.), it may either be a present payment or a sum the husband must pay his wife if he divorces her without cause. A deferred dowry, therefore, is one of the stratagems to save a daughter from the polygamous instincts of man. Another is to require the pronouncement of a *ta'alik* or admission of automatic divorce if a second wife be taken. It is in fact often the practice among Malays and Indians to require a bridegroom at his marriage to say, "If I take another wife or if I absent myself six months on land or a year at sea without sending letter or money to my wife, she is automatically divorced". This is one kind of divorce by mutual consent, when the husband who has to pronounce this promise may yet escape the financial consequences of a contested divorce. But Muhammadan law tries to discourage separation. A Malay may say "I divorce you" once or twice, and make it up with his wife, but if he says then or thereafter "I divorce you for a third time", the parties have to be remarried, which is permitted only if the woman has been wedded and bedded by another. A man may thus divorce and remarry his wife twice, but not oftener, a third divorce being irrevocable. A woman can obtain a judicial divorce (*pasah*) for desertion or continued failure by her husband to provide maintenance. But being more volatile than man, she is restrained from demanding divorce for any other reason such as jealousy or dislike by having to restore her dowry or perhaps even double her dowry (*tebus talak* or *khula* Ar.). Even then the husband, however reluctantly, must be persuaded to pronounce the divorce. A procedure

---

[1] *Mas kahwin*, once the term for bride-price is now the Malay term for the Muslim *mahr*.

so expensive and so uncertain is rare, the average wife preferring to exasperate her husband till he divorces her.

The Malay family is neither patriarchal, in the sense of children belonging to the father's family; nor, outside Negri Sembilan, matrilineal in the sense of children belonging to the mother's tribe; the constitution of the family is parental, children belonging to both parents. The Ninety-Nine Laws of Perak give the practice obtaining there in the 18th century. "If the child of divorced parents is under nine years of age, it will live with the mother, if it is over nine, it can please itself whether it lives with its father or its mother, but a girl should live with her mother." The parental system is governed by what the Malays call "Temenggong custom". And observers have concluded perhaps wrongly that it exhibits traces of a former matrilineal system. There is the old custom of a young husband living for a while with his wife's family. And the Ninety-Nine Laws, just quoted, lay down that when a person dies "house and garden, crockery, kitchen utensils and bedding are to be taken by the female children, iron tools or weapons, rice-fields and mines by the sons". These rules were still in force when the British entered Perak. "In that state," wrote Sir William Maxwell in 1884, "the lands and houses of the deceased descend to his daughters equally, while the sons divide the personal property, being expected to acquire land for themselves by clearing and planting it or by marrying women who have inherited it". And an official has recorded how two decades ago (and almost certainly still), in the southern districts of Perak "where the family agreed on the distribution of an inheritance, the result was usually to give a specific piece of land to the widow or dependent daughter and for sons to share equally with daughters or even to waive altogether in favour of daughters. Sometimes they would agree to give the whole estate to their mother, no doubt on the understanding that she would not sell it, thus in effect postponing distribution till after the death of both parents." One may suspect the influence of the Hindu, who commonly deferred the division of a deceased father's

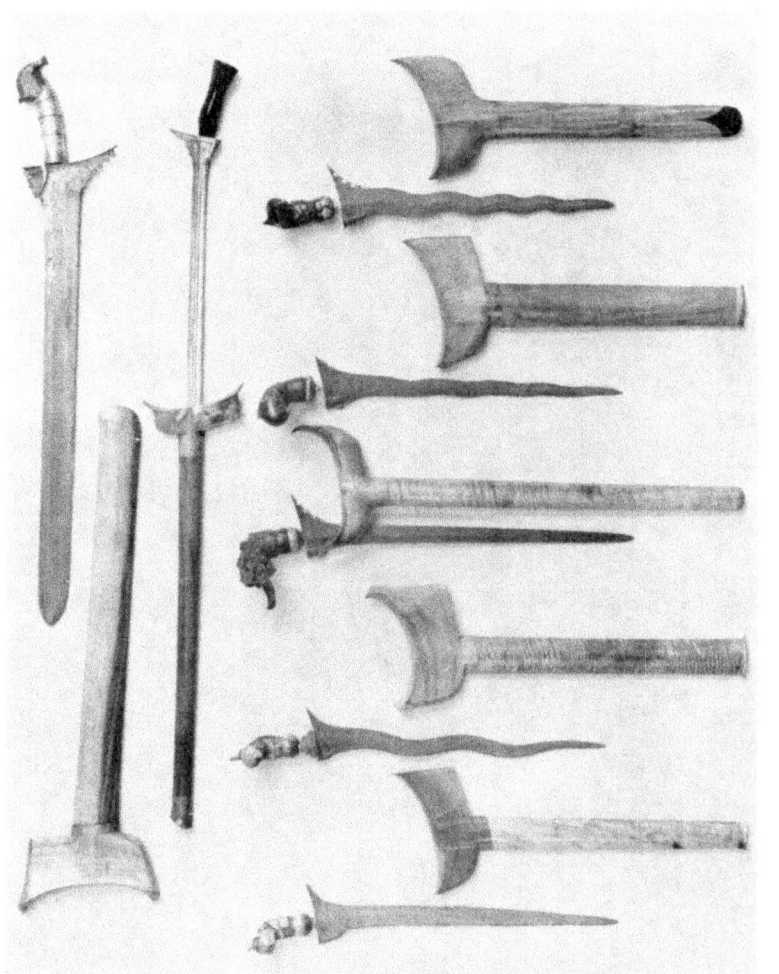

Malay Weapons

property until the widow had died and no longer needed support. Anyhow, among the Malays it appears still to be the usual practice. Advantage is taken of a provision of Muslim law that the distribution of estates can be settled by consent of the heirs, and Malay commonsense has prevailed over the Muslim allotment of a mere eighth of the property to the widow, a portion suited perhaps to conditions in Arabia, but too small for a Malay widow's subsistence. Before the British advised in the administration of Malay States, titles to land were not registered there, and when registration started the tendency was to register them in the names of women. Apart from the general respect for women's rights in the Malay world, it may be remembered that in the 15th century Malacca was in close touch with two Sumatran districts, Siak and Indragiri, where Minangkabau matrilineal influence was strong. Then for 200 years most of the immigrants into Malaya were Bugis, whose womenfolk in Celebes enjoy equal rights to property with men, take part in public affairs and have often been elected to fill a throne. In Perak Achinese influence was paramount during most of the 17th century, and in Acheh "houses and homesteads were as a rule assigned to daughters and rice-fields and weapons to sons".

It is a pity that the parental system of inheritance in Malaya has received far less attention than the matrilineal system of Negri Sembilan, and it is probable that a proper survey might reveal variations in different States.

At any rate, it is clear that among the Malays women can hardly be described as an inferior sex, although immemorial superstition makes it rare for the unsophisticated to feed with their male folk, and Muhammadan law is less kind to them over divorce and inheritance than native custom. Even in a matter like the abolition of slavery, Raja Idris, afterwards Sultan of Perak, released his own slaves but apologized for his inability to free slaves who were the personal property of his wife. The income, too, of a Muhammadan woman from her own private property or settlements is independent of control by her husband. One of the features of peasant life in Kelantan that struck Dr. Raymond Firth when he was making his valuable study of the fishing community there was "the freedom of the women especially in economic matters. Not only do they exercise an important influence on the control of the family finances, commonly acting as bankers for their husbands, but they also engage in independent enterprises, which increase the family supply of cash. Petty trading in fish and vegetables, the preparation and sale of various forms of snacks and cooked fish, mat-making, spinning and net-making, harvesting rice, tile-making, the preparation of coconut-oil, the selling of small groceries in shops are some of the occupations followed by women. . . . At least 25 per cent. of the adult women of this community have some definite occupation that yields a regular income. And if casual or intermittent work is also taken into consideration—such as selling a husband's fish, fish-gutting, etc., probably some 50 per cent. of the adult women are gainfully employed from time to time." Many are teachers in vernacular schools. A Malay woman does all the house-work, cooks, sews and looks after her children. She also plants out rice and reaps it. She may be a weaver. She may work on the home garden, or she may angle. If there is alluvial mining near, she may wash for tin or gold, or she may tap rubber on her own land or as a wage-earner on an estate. Heavy work is done by men. They plough the rice-fields, build houses and make fences, build boats, are smiths and sea-fishermen.

Malay society, however, if without much differentiation between the sexes, is by no means without class distinctions. The main distinction is between raja and commoner, but within both these classes there are degrees. A raja of royal descent on both sides (*waris benēh dan tanah* or *anak gahara*) is of higher rank than one with a commoner mother (*waris benēh*), and in theory and generally in practice had a claim above primogeniture to succeed to a throne. Contrariwise, an old title, borne by the first princely ruler of Malacca to signify that his consort was of higher degree than himself, was Parameswara, and by coincidence this title was revived in Perak by the title of Permaisuri for the commoner wife of a Sultan. For a Malay Raja may marry a woman of any class, although for his first bride he is expected to take a lady of his own rank. If he married a woman of inferior birth, it was customary for him not to attend the wedding in person but to follow the Hindu practice of sending his headkerchief or creese to represent him. Yet the children of a male raja by any wife, even a negress, are styled rajas. Hindu law allowed three wives for a Brahmin, two for a Kshatriya and one for the Vaisya. Similarly, polygamy was a symbol of rank in old Malay society, although nowadays even a ruler will often not have more than one wife at a time. In Negri Sembilan, custom prescribed that only the Yang di-pertuan (or Ruler) could have four wives, only an Undang or territorial chief three, only a Lembaga or tribal chief two, and ordinary folk one.

While a Malay raja could marry a person of any rank, that liberty was not enjoyed by his women folk, who were socially degraded unless they married a raja or a sayid, that is, a descendant of the Prophet. Originally in Pasai and then in Malacca, Kedah and Perak the son of a marriage between a commoner and a raja lady bore the title of Megat from the Sanskrit Magadha, the son of a Vaisya father by a Kshatriya mother, and a daughter had the now obsolete title of Putri. The title Megat became hereditary in the male line. But the '*Adat Raja-Raja Melayu* from 18th century Malacca gives a curious declension on the female side, which if it is authentic could have obtained only in the Malayo-Javanese society of mediaeval Malacca. The passage runs:—"If a Megat's sister marry beneath her, for example a Mantri, her sons are *biduanda*. If a *biduanda*'s sister marry a commoner, her son is a *kshatriya*" (that is of the second or warrior and princely caste of the Hindu). "If a *kshatriya*'s sister marry a commoner, her son has the Javanese title of *periai*. If a *periai*'s sister marry a commoner, her son is a *perwira*. If a *perwira*'s sister marry a commoner, her son is a *sida*. If a *sida*'s son marry a commoner, her son is a *hulubalang*," or captain, a fitting title for males of *kshatriya* descent. The passage continues. "Such are the rules of descent. But the sons of the four Mantri are all styled *biduanda* and a ruler's pages can be called *kshatriya*, especially as they may be of noble birth and heirs of Mantri Penggawah." If these obsolete classes denote an embryonic caste system, Islam extinguished it.

In Celebes when a man of lower rank marries a girl of high descent, he can purchase nobility for himself and his children. An echo of this system is to be found in the Ninety-Nine Laws of Perak, though there the custom is prescribed not for raja ladies but for Sharifahs (or female descendants of the Prophet):—"It is not permissible for a woman of the Hashimites to wed an ordinary person, but if the ordinary person pay five *paha* of gold in consideration of his low birth, then the marriage can take place." Even to-day throughout the Malay States so much obloquy attaches to the mes-alliance of a raja lady, that such a match is generally runaway and leads to emigration to another state.

In addition to distinctions of birth, the Malays recognized distinction due to religion, trade or profession, personal characteristics and civic status. By mediaeval theory only a Christian could be a member of a Christian state, and in days before British protection only a Muslim could have proprietary rights over Malay land. Moreover, though he is no longer aware of the source of his Hindu prejudice, the Malay has followed the code of Manu in regarding medicine-men, usurers, sailors, dancers, one-eyed persons and those with thick hair on their bodies as people to be avoided when it comes to marriage. From this Hindu ban the modern doctor is not only excluded, but he is regarded on account of his means as an eligible young man.

Then there were slaves. The "Malay Annals" relate how the Bendahara or Prime Minister of the last Sultan of Malacca had so many slaves that if one of them arrived smartly dressed he would be mistaken for a stranger and invited up into the house, until his identity was discovered and he was ordered to sit down below. Aristocratic circles will even now look down upon the descendants of those who before the abolition of slavery some seventy years ago belonged to the class of slaves by purchase, capture or indebtedness. About the year 1911, one of the Rulers complained that such undesirables were being admitted to the Malay Eton, though enquiry revealed that their admission had been at the request of his own relatives, who had exhibited a feudal generosity towards the children of their retainers.

Slavery was a feature of Malay life before the coming of the Hindus, existing among primitive tribes like the Mois in Indo-China, where debt slavery was common. When the British started to administer Perak, they found not only debt-bondsmen but four kinds of slave proper, namely (1) captives taken in war, (2) pagans like the Sakai who were hunted down and captured, (3) manslayers and other criminals who unable to pay the price of blood surrendered themselves and family to the Raja as slaves (*ulor* in the first generation, *alar* if born in slavery) and (4) the children of a female slave other than any acknowledged as his by her owner. To these had to be added Abyssinian and negro slaves brought back from Mecca by wealthy pilgrims. The number of slaves bought appears not to have been large. In 1790 only nine were imported into Penang, in 1791 seven, in 1792 forty-six, the average price being forty Spanish dollars a head. In Newbold's day about twenty Batak slaves were imported annually into Sungai Ujong. Yet the number of slaves (*hamba*, '*abdi*) and debt-bondsmen (*orang berutang*, *hamba*, *kawan*) in Perak about 1874 was estimated at 3,000 or a sixteenth of the then population. "The ownership of a number of slaves and debt-bondsmen was a mark of a man of rank, wealth and influence."

The slaves of the Ruler were a special class. To strike one of them wrongfully involved the penalty of death, and any person who enticed one away had to make good fourteen times his value. Besides having slaves by purchase or inheritance, those born in his household and those who in search of sanctuary preferred servitude to death, the former Sultans of Perak (and of other States too) could formerly carry off all the young women of districts with no great chief to protect them in order to recruit maids or wet-nurses on the occasion of a royal marriage or birth. In Perak, districts for this kind of *battue* were Kampar, Sungkai and Pulau Tiga. If a girl was married, her husband accompanied her into bondage. If she was unmarried, usually she became a courtesan about the palace, and if she were allowed to marry, the dower went to the Raja, and her husband became a royal slave. The tortures inflicted on royal slaves in Pahang have been described by Sir Hugh Clifford.

Most iniquitous of all was the system of debt-slavery, a system alien to Islamic law, but occurring in various forms among the Hindus. At law, a debt-bondsman was a free man (*merdehēka*) whose liberty in Perak could be purchased theoretically for $25 (100 *bidor*). Nor in theory could any man be fined more than that sum. Actually redemption for $25 was often refused, and far higher fines than $25 were often imposed. "The desire to possess some particular persons sometimes led to the invention of fictitious debts, and people were liable with little hope of redress to be dragged from their homes, nominally as security for some debt of which perhaps they had never heard. No work that debt-bondsmen performed for their creditors and masters operated to lessen the debt. They served in his household, cultivated his fields and worked in his mines; but such service was merely a necessary incident of their position and was not accepted in part payment. Sometimes the master fed and clothed them, more often they had to supply themselves with all necessaries notwithstanding that their labour was forfeited to the master's service."

Again, in spite of the rule that the wife and children of a debtor should not be liable for his debt, unless it were incurred with their knowledge, and that the widow of a debt-bondsman should not be liable for more than a third of her husband's debt, creditors would often hold the wife and family of a debtor in bondage for the full amount during his life-time and after his death. The daughters of a debt-bondsman were given in marriage by the creditor, who took the dower or held the bridegroom in bondage till he could pay it. No part of such a dower went towards the extinction of the girl's family debt. "This monstrous injustice," in Sir William Maxwell's view, was "of modern introduction or there would be few but debt-bondsmen among the population. It has been imitated from the analogous practice in the case of slaves (*'abdi*) but is an unauthorized and illegal innovation. Another rule, frequently evaded in Perak, gave to any female debtor with whom her master cohabited an absolute right to the cancelment of her debt, and made the master punishable by fine if he did not give the woman her freedom." Under Muhammadan law a slave is not allowed to inherit or make a will, but though despised, Malay debt-bondsmen were not subject to any of the legal disabilities of slaves proper. Our knowledge of debt slavery comes from digests of Malay law supplemented by the studies of Sir William Maxwell, an official concerned in the abolition of slavery in the Malay States.

As in Siam, Burma and Ceylon, even the free cultivator was not exempt from feudal service to his overlords as one of the conditions of tenancy. "In a Malay state," writes Sir William Maxwell in 1884, "the exaction of personal service from the *ra'ayat* is limited only by the powers of endurance of the latter. The superior authority is obliged from self-interest to stop short of the point at which oppression will compel the cultivator to abandon his land and emigrate. But within this limit the cultivator may be required to give his labour in making roads, bridges, drains and other works of public utility, to tend elephants, to pole boats, to carry letters and messages, to attend his chief when travelling, to cultivate his chief's fields as well as his own and to serve as a soldier when required. Local custom often regulates the kind of service exacted from the cultivator in a particular district. Thus in Perak one district used to supply the Raja with timber for building purposes, while rattans and other materials came from others; the people of one locality used to furnish the musicians for the Raja's band, while another had to provide nurses and attendants for his children." Speaking of Kedah, Colonel Low says, "The ryot was obliged to pay for keeping up bands of music and state elephants. His children were liable to be forcibly taken from him—the girls for the seraglio and the youths for public works or for war, where they got no pay and but precarious supplies of food."

The *kerah* or corvée was organized by the village headman at the orders of his chief or raja. He fined the recalcitrant and took money from those able to buy exemption, following the Malay adage that when one bows to a raja's mandate one can hug one's own interest under one's arm. But while under a just chief there was no grumbling, no circumstance of Malay rule did more to swell the population of Penang and Province Wellesley in the old days, immigrants being willing to abandon and forfeit their land rather than endure unjust exactions in Kedah and Patani. Yet the right to demand reasonable feudal service in return for occupation of land was indisputable and justified a reasonable land rent in return for its abrogation. And when the British first went into Perak the difficulty of finding labour for public works led them to require gratuitous labour for six days every year from all Malay males above 15 and below 50 except Rajas, farmers paying rent to the State or one official of each kind attached to a mosque (*Imam, Khatib, Bilal, Siak*). Exemption might be bought at the rate of 25 cents a day. But even before forced labour was abolished, British influence had led to a general strike by the peasantry against a system they had formerly accepted.

II Matrilineal

Except that descent for the Rajas is patrilineal and that Rajas and chiefs had slaves, the social system in Negri

Sembilan is entirely different from that of all the other Malay States.

Mother-right has provided the rules for succession and inheritance among American Indians, among the Khassis whom a late migration carried to Assam about 2000 B.C., and among the Minangkabaus of Sumatra and Negri Sembilan in a form so academically perfect as to delight the ardent anthropologist more than the busy magistrate or land officer. It exists among many other races. The matrilineal system of the Chams of Indo-China has been compared with that of the Minangkabaus. Mother-right is observed in parts of Melanesia and among the Nayars of Malabar.

Among the Khassis many tribes almost deify the ancestresses from whom they trace their descent. In the Minangkabau parts of Negri Sembilan the names of the ancestresses of many tribes and sub-tribes are recorded in folk-lore, and the grave of the mother of the first Penghulu of Muar is a sacred place. There were, however, several obstacles to the worship of an ancestress in Negri Sembilan. Not only was the Minangkabau immigration comparatively recent, but the country down to the 18th century was under the Bendaharas or Prime Ministers of the kingdom of Malacca and its successor Johor, and the Bendaharas ruled the Nine Counties through patriarchal chiefs. Again, when the Minangkabau colonists arrived, the great bulk of the population was Proto-Malay. Some of the colonists may have married these pagan aborigines, and anyhow their matrilineal system or custom of the Patihs ('*adat perpatih*) led the Minangkabaus to invent a title to the land through aboriginal females. Yet to worship a pagan aborigine, whether real or fictitious, was beyond even the laxest Muslim.

Among the Minangkabaus as among the Khassis there are exogamous tribes, called *suku* in Negri Sembilan, and sub-tribes that are called "the womb" (*kpoh* Kh. = *perut* N.S.) by both peoples. The word for tribe (*suku*) means literally quarter, and it has been surmised that a Minangkabau state or county arose from the commingling of four tribes, two of which had the *jus connubii* with the other two. In Negri Sembilan multiples of four obsessed the framers of the Rembau constitution and are popular everywhere. Most of the tribes of Negri Sembilan brought Minangkabau names from their Sumatran homeland and these were for convenience often territorial: a man might belong to the Banyan-Tree sub-tribe of the Flat Plain tribe. As time passed there were new sub-divisions due to local settlements and migrations, such as the "Sri Lemak tribe that came from Minangkabau" and the "Sri Lemak tribe from Pahang" or "the Biduanda tribes from Sungai Ujong".

Among some Indonesian peoples, though not among the Malays of the Padang highlands, the first tribe to inhabit a state is supreme over the others. So, in Negri Sembilan the Biduanda is the premier tribe, the name being an honorific applied by 15th century Sultans of Malacca to noblemen with a dash of royal blood on the maternal side, and also to early Chinese settlers and to a Proto-Malay group. A section of the Biduanda tribe (which the Minangkabaus created after the matriarchal model and in time enlarged) was evidently from early patriarchal Malacca exploiters of the hinterland, and the few families descended from those pioneers still provide the big territorial chiefs of Negri Sembilan and alone deserve the title of *waris* or "heirs" of the land. No doubt their ancestors stressed or invented royal descent on the distaff side to suit Minangkabau matrilineal ideas. Anyhow, their importance was recognized. No Minangkabau could attach *waris* land or demand a member of the *waris* in substitution for a Minangkabau murdered by a *waris*. But if a *waris* was killed by a Minangkabau, the slayer's tribe had to give five persons as substitutes.

The inability of two tribes or sub-tribes to trace descent from a common ancestress is their sanction for intermarriage. A Khassi could commit no greater sin than to marry within his matrilineal tribe or sub-tribe, and in Negri Sembilan outlawry and confiscation of property used to be the penalties for incest as such a marriage was termed. In Negri Sembilan putting "two ladders against one sugar-palm", that is, marriage or a liaison during a wife's life with another woman of her tribe was punishable with death, but both for Minangkabaus and Khassis marriage with a deceased wife's sister is a common practice, as it makes for the welfare of the children of the wife's tribe. Among both peoples the marriage of the children of sisters is of course prohibited, but the children of a brother and sister can intermarry, as belonging to two different maternal tribes. Among both peoples, illogically, the marriage of the children of brothers, although through their mothers they may belong to different tribes, is forbidden—the modern fiction in Negri Sembilan being that on the decease of a father the uncle becomes his niece's guardian (*wali*) and on the decease of father and uncle, the male cousin becomes her guardian and therefore unable to marry her, an objection not raised by Muslim law. On divorce the Minangkabau like the Khassi mother has custody of the children. Among the Khassis polygamy is said not to exist, and in spite of Islam and wealth from rubber booms the Minangkabau generally prefers monogamy, which is the surest guarantee that a tribeswoman and her children will be supported. "A second marriage destroys half the man's value as a tribal asset."

Among the Minangkabaus as among the Khassis the head of a married household is the wife's eldest brother, and a husband is under his wife's tribal officer so far as she and her children are concerned: he is a lodger in his wife's house though he may be a tribal officer for his own tribe.

Not until the political system of the Minangkabaus and their tribal law of property come to be described, will all the consequences and advantages of belonging to a tribe be apparent. But in the figurative language of the Minangkabaus clearly there would be no place in their country for a stranger who did not "bellow" mother-right in their "byre" or "bleat" exogamy in their "pen". So a Minangkabau woman might adopt a person of either sex, of any age and of any race into her tribe. Full adoption (*'adat dan pesaka*) gives a woman (and her children whether born before or after the adoption) all the rights of inheritance and all the responsibilities belonging to the natural daughters and grand-daughters of her adopter. A man, if fully adopted, becomes eligible for office in his adopting tribe. When in the old days a tribe had to provide a murdered person's tribe with a substitute for the dead, in order to make that substitution complete, the child given was admitted to the rights of full adoption. Limited adoption (*'adat pada lembaga*) of a girl of one's own tribe or sub-tribe gives her a right only to property expressly declared and bestowed during the life of the adopting mother. Limited adoption of a girl from another tribe was very rare, as it cut her off from her own tribal property and privileges; so, too, limited adoption of a man from another tribe was too damaging to his prospects for it ever to occur. Limited adoption of a foreigner was a preliminary to his settling among Minangkabaus and marrying a tribeswoman, so that he might be subject to the jurisdiction of some tribal chief: he could then commit "incest" by violating the rule of exogamy but he got no vote, was ineligible for tribal office and could not have even a life interest in ancestral land.

How in their social and economic effects do the matrilineal and patriarchal systems compare? In Negri Sembilan as elsewhere women hold no office, possess no executive authority and have no right to enter into any contract, even a marriage contract. But unlike their sisters in patriarchal states they enjoy the vote for the election of tribal officers, and the registration of tribal lands in their names gives them so much comparative affluence and freedom that the marriage tie is looser in Negri Sembilan than in other states.

Among primitive Indonesian peoples marriage was an

arrangement for the benefit of two families, and where the bridegroom's relatives came to pay (not the bride but) the bride's relatives for her hand, more or less equivalent presents or a house or maintenance for the couple were given in return. But under the old Minangkabau custom a bridegroom enjoyed two advantages. For, in the first place, as a potential asset to his wife's tribe, he had to pay no brideprice. And, in the second place, for him to labour on his wife's fields instead of those of his mother or sisters was in theory a supererogation of marital duty. Islam, however, has compelled the man to pay not indeed a bride-price but a dowry to his wife, which however she may prefer to leave in abeyance as she has under Muslim law to repay it two-fold should she divorce him. And divorce is all the more likely on account of the attitude of her relatives to her husband, in spite of tribal theory. A Jelebu tribal saying puts it frankly:—

> When a man marries and goes to his wife's family,
> If clever, he will be a friend in council;
> If a fool, he will be ordered here and there;
> A tall man, he will be as a sheltering buttress;
> Prosperous, he will be as a laden branch that gives shade.
> The married man must go or stay as he is bid. . . .
> If he is learned, he shall pray for us,
> If rich, we will use his gold;
> If lame, he shall scare our chicken,
> If blind, he shall pound our rice-mortars,
> If deaf, he shall fire our cannon.
> When you enter a byre, low;
> When you enter a goat's pen, bleat;
> Follow the customs of your wife's family. . . .
> A bridegroom among his wife's relations
> Is like a soft cucumber among spiny durian;
> If he rolls against them, he is hurt,
> And he's hurt if they roll against him.[1]

It is clear that the success of a marriage under such conditions depends largely on the willingness of the man to be

[1] See Appendix A, p. 183.

an economic asset to his wife's tribe. Yet financial considerations must make him chary of separation. Now that Islam has introduced the dowry, a man if he divorces his wife for anything but adultery loses it. On divorce the woman of course retains all her tribal property, and any property acquired and developed by the joint labour of the married pair is by custom divided equally. Yet the matrilineal system hardly encourages a husband to struggle to develop pre-marital personal property. For on his death it goes under the custom not to his own children, who are of his wife's tribe, but to his sisters or sisters' children who are members of his own tribe. And though the abolition of slavery has robbed the man of the greatest benefit of the matrilineal system, namely that his tribe being responsible for his expenses he could not become a debt-bondsman, even now it is to his own female relatives that he turns in the hour of need. On the whole perhaps the matrilineal system still benefits the male, though it dulls some of the normal incentives to industry. Certainly there are two strong points in its favour. It shuts the door on the Indian moneylender. And sharpening their wits on the sayings that enshrine tribal law the people are some of the most intelligent in the peninsula. British bureaucracy has scotched but certainly not killed the perfect pattern of democracy which the Minangkabaus of Negri Sembilan cherish.[1]

---

[1] A Minangkabau digest from Perak (Maxwell Malay MS.44 in the Library of the Royal Asiatic Society, London) states that the birth of twins, if boy and girl, is an impropriety (*sumbang*). The headman must collect followers, discharge gunpowder (*bedil*) at the parents' house and seize some of their possessions such as sugar, rice or bananas. He must capture the twins for the father to redeem. So is disaster averted.

5: POLITICAL SYSTEMS

I Patriarchal

THE head and cornerstone of the Malay State (*negeri* = *nagara* Skt.), itself a Hindu concept, is the ruler, Yang di-pertuan "He who is made lord" to give him his Malay title, Raja to retain his Hindu style, or Sultan to employ the Muslim description. And research has confirmed the truth of folk-lore in the "Malay Annals" that the origin of this Malay royalty was due to the marriage of Indian immigrants with the daughters of local chiefs, their children inheriting Hindu ideas of territory and divinity grafted on to primitive Malay conceptions of the tribe and of the magical power of chiefs and medicine-men. Tomé Pires tells how eighteen Celates (or proto-Malays who lived partly on land and partly in boats on the *Selat* or Straits) went to Parameswara, first ruler of Malacca, to remind him it was their advice that had led to his removal from Muar to Bertam, where he lived before founding a settlement at Malacca. "They asked him to fulfil his promise and reward them with some gift of honour, on which petition the said Parameswara made them mandarins—which means nobles—them and their sons and their wives for ever. Hence it is that all the mandarins of Malacca are descended from these, and the kings are descended through the female side, according to what is said in the country." This royal descent may be a survival of a matrilineal system.

Ideas of the magical powers of chiefs older than the Hindu are still extant in the Malay world. The custom in Japan and formerly in Malaya of vacating the palace of a dead king and starting a new capital, the practice of giving deceased rulers in ancient China as in Malaya posthumous titles, the couch-throne used in Japan's oldest enthronement ritual and in parts of Indonesia, the reverence for regalia without which no Japanese or Malay can become a ruler, all these would appear to belong to a very early layer of civilisation. The Indonesian Dayak believes that at first the Creator stretched out the heavens no bigger than a mango, and a medicine-woman in a Dayak legend satisfies an army with rice steamed in a pot the size of a chestnut and with meat cooked in a pan the size of a bird's nest. The heads of the Perak royal drums are fabled to be the skins of lice and the royal clarionet to be made of a nettle stalk. The pillars of the palace of the Sultan of Minangkabau were fashioned of nettle-stalks and the Sultan possessed a dagger formed of the soul of steel, coeval with creation. The Malay ruler therefore like the Malay magician was a master of the mannikin soul of things. And if, as seems certain, ideas derive from great centres of civilisation, then this conception of the power of Malay kings will have come in prehistoric times to the Malays, as to China in the Chou period 3000 years ago, from Babylon or some other centre in the Middle East, to be carried from Yunnan down to the archipelago, a conception that developed centuries later into the idea of a Malay king having in his veins the white blood of a Hindu god or of a Boddhisatva and finally of a Muslim saint.

The office of shaman, like that of ruler, is often hereditary among Malays, and both possess as insignia drums and tambourines baleful to those who touch them, though the ruler's vengeful instruments have become part of a Muslim's *naubat* band. As late as 1874 Perak folk saw nothing strange in their Sultan, 'Abdu'llah, sitting at a *séance* on the shaman's mat and becoming possessed by the genies of the State, who prophesied the death of a British Resident destined soon to be murdered. Just as Japan had a spiritual head in the Mikado and a secular in the Shogun, so however it came by him, Perak had in addition to its secular ruler a Sultan Muda or State Shaman, whose duty it was annually to refresh the regalia by proffering them food and drink and on occasion to sacrifice to the guardian spirits of the country, brought within the fold of Muslim orthodoxy by inclusion under djinns who are all subservient to Allah.

While the rulers of Malay port kingdoms waxed rich on tolls and dues, it is perhaps significant that like the shaman (and the Khassi chief) a Yang di-pertuan of inland Minangkabau or Negri Sembilan had no source of income beyond the produce of the royal demesne and voluntary contributions for ceremonial functions. But though the Malay shaman frequently uses a tabu vocabulary, there appear to be no words reserved for him and his actions, like those Hinduism has reserved for the Malay king. In that old Indonesian tongue, Sundanese, the words *siram* "bathe", *gering* "dry = sick", *ulu* "head", *berangkat* "be carried = travel", *titah* "order", *mangkat* "borne away, dead" are not as in Malaya reserved for royalty and tabu for others; and the words "be carried" for the royal mode of progression, "borne away" as a euphemism for death, and "dry" for "sick" embody Hindu ideas that a king must never set foot on earth, and his subjects must never allude to him as subject to mortality. Along with those Indonesian words tabu in Malaya for all but royalty have been joined the Sanskrit terms *murka* "angry", *kurnia* "gift", *anugrah* "give". For to graft the Hindu conception of a divine king on to the Indonesian master of magic was in many respects easy. A man might be born a shaman or he might be made one by magic rites, just as a Hindu king, though hereditary, acquired divinity by the performance of the magic ritual of enthronement, which under a Muslim veneer is still for Malays a Hindu and Buddhist ceremony.

As in Vedic ritual and as still at enthronements in Cambodia and Siam, the initial steps at a Malay enthronement are to wash away the old man by lustration and to anoint the new; though nowadays these two steps are sometimes confused and merged into one. Next, wearing necklet and armlets like a Hindu god, the Sultan of Perak has thrust into his headdress a mediaeval "lightning" seal (*chap halilintar*), whose handle is made of "thunder" (*gempita*) wood that "causes matter to fly"; and this seal must have taken the place of Indra's *vajra* or thunderbolt symbol so often represented in Indian and Javanese sculpture. In Vedic times an Indian king was given at his enthronement a wooden sword termed a thunderbolt as a weapon against demons. And when the Perak Sultan sat enthroned, a court herald of Brahmin origin would read a formula in corrupt Sanskrit lauding his victory (over evil), his luck, his justice and his power of healing. After that address a new Malay ruler, like a Hindu king, promises to rule justly in accordance with law.

A feature of the ritual whose significance has been forgotten is the immobility the ruler is expected to preserve, such stillness being evidence in Hindu ritual of incipient godhead. And as for godhead, although the titles of pre-Muslim rulers have generally perished, the Tamil poem Manimekalai mentions two Malay kings who claimed descent from Indra. Bhisma states that when a Hindu king is crowned, it is Indra who is crowned and anyone who desires prosperity should worship him as Indra is worshipped. The capitals of Pahang and of a Sumatran State were called Indrapura or "towns of Indra". The hill behind the Sri Menanti palace in Negri Sembilan is the Hill of Sri Indra. Sailendras were "Indra of the mountain". It was not only of Indra that Indonesian kings became the mortal receptacles. The tomb of the founder of Majapahit (A.D. 1294–1300) shows this Javanese ruler sculptured as Vishnu, and his principal wife was represented as Parvati. The famous sacrificial knife of the Minangkabau regalia, the "blade from the lake Mandakini on the heaven-born Ganges", has inlaid figures of Aditiavarman, a 14th century ruler of Minangkabau and of his wife as a Bhairava and his *sakti*, that is, as one of the terrible manifestations of the god Siva and his consort Mahadewi. But Indra as master of the weather, lord of lightning and bestower of rain, whose bow is the rainbow, was a popular object of worship among agricultural people like the Malays and not being immortal was accepted by Buddhists.

The heaven over which Indra ruled, Shurga, with its

cities of gods and celestial spirits is situated on Meru, the Olympus of the Hindus, a fabulous mountain at the navel of the earth, and Meru or Maha-Meru "the great Meru" plays a prominent part in Malay folk-lore. The Indonesian respect for high places is attested by pyramids (like Java's Chandi Sukuh) built under some influence that appears to have come from Mesopotamia long before Hindus brought their architecture to the Malay world. Herodotus tells how there was as much of the tower of Babel below ground as above, and the same idea is perpetuated in the Hindu conception of Mount Meru, in the sculpture of Bayon and in Java's Barabudur where a row of bas-reliefs depicting the lower world of desire and sensual pleasure was buried under the earth. The conception of a cosmic mountain spread through Asia very early. As Confucius reminds us, even five centuries before Christ, there was "an earth-mound at the borders of a Chinese town or village, interpreted as symbolizing the whole soil of the territory in which it stood." The Malays must have had a similar belief in their home-land of Yunnan, and centuries later when they became Hindus they turned this mound into a miniature Meru and held that every king was lord of the realm by virtue of possessing one. In the museum at Jakarta there was (and may still be) a sculptured Meru being transported by the gods from India to Java. The rulers of Sri Vijaya were associated with a Maha-Meru in Palembang. In Burma, Siam, Indo-China and Indonesia, the capitals of old kingdoms in sequence from a more ancient symbol had like Angkor a hillock or like Angkor Thom a Buddhist shrine or like Bali a Hindu temple or like Mandalay a palace tower, all of them identified with Mount Meru. The owner of such a hill, temple or palace was a receptacle or incarnation of Siva or Vishnu or Indra; always of Indra where Hinayana Buddhism admitted no immortal god, the long-lived lord of Meru being the best substitute. No wonder Siamese and Malays closed their umbrellas when passing a palace that was the abode of an incarnate god or of a Boddhisatva or his worldly counterpart, a Chakravartin. And a part of the enthronement ceremonies in Siam and in Malaya was the procession by the new ruler round his Meru, whether hill or palace, a symbolic taking possession of his kingdom in little. On the fifth day of the Cambodian enthronement ritual princes and dignitaries forming a circle about the king pass round nineteen times from left to right seven disks set on tapers, whose smoke they fan towards him. This ceremony symbolizes the revolution of the seven planets about Mount Meru, here represented by the king.

Strangely enough to modern minds the astrological notions centring round this Hindu Olympus actually affected the political structure of Siam, Cambodia and Malay States, and was and is even still of practical importance. In old Malacca, modern Perak, Kedah, Pahang and Negri Sembilan there was the same preoccupation with the astrological numbers 4, 8, 16 and 32 that has been traced in Burma, Siam and Cambodia. Generally in all those countries there were four chief ministers, and four chief consorts for the rulers. At his enthronement a king of Siam or Cambodia is surrounded by eight Brahmins representing the Lokapalas who guard the eight points of the Brahmin cosmogony. In Kedah and Perak and Pahang there are 4 great chiefs and 8 major chiefs and even the ground-plan of an old Perak palace shows pillars in four sets of 8, making 32 for each main section of the building. The regalia of the ruler of Negri Sembilan comprise 8 tufted spears, 8 swords, 8 creeses, 8 large candles, 8 small tapers, 8 betel boxes, 8 handfuls of ashes, 8 water-vessels, 16 pennons and 16 umbrellas. In Negri Sembilan and probably in other states salutes numbered 8, 16 and 32. For part of his coronation a king of Siam sits on an octagonal throne, and fifty years ago when a shaman's *séance* was being conducted to cure his illness, a sick Sultan of Perak was seated on a sixteen-sided throne to await with shrouded head and grass-brush in hand the advent of the spirits of the realm. Pegu in the 14th century had thirty-two provinces whose governors with the king made up the number of the gods in Indra's mountain paradise. In Pahang and Kedah besides 4 great and 8 major there are 16 minor chiefs. Perak and old Malacca, besides 4 great, 8 major and 16 minor chiefs, boast also of 32 petty territorial chiefs. "A passage in the New History of the T'ang Dynasty," Dr. von Heine-Geldern has noted, "indicates that the kingdom of Java in the 9th century was divided into 28 provinces, their governors together with the four ministers again having numbered 32 high officials. This may have been a somewhat older form of the same system, in which the provinces corresponded to constellations, the 28 Houses of the Moon, and the 4 ministers to the guardian gods of the cardinal points. It is clear that in all these cases the empire was conceived as an image of the heavenly world of stars and gods." "The magician before time existed was Allah and He revealed Himself by the light of moon and sun and so showed Himself to be verily a magician." There is the Malay's latest synthesis.

Before that, syncretism in the Hindu period saw Father Sky turn into Indra, lord of Meru and controller of weather, a change commemorated in such Minangkabau sayings as:

> He the first Raja primaeval,
> Dropped he as the rain from heaven. . . .
> White the blood that in him flowed.

And victor also over evil, the Malay ruler is associated with light. The Perak enthronement address (*chiri*) talks of the new king "ravishing the three worlds by the jewels of his crown". The Kedah regalia include a looking glass, termed the Sunbeam, on a pole. No Malay but a ruler may use a white or yellow umbrella, wear yellow raiment or have yellow house-furnishings or daggers mounted with bright gold or golden anklets. And the Raja claimed as his perquisites albino birds, albino animals and albino children.

As study of Malay legal systems reveals, the penalties for offences against royalty were heavy and deterrent. According to the Malacca digest of A.D. 1450, if a sea-captain abducted a royal slave, he was liable to be executed; if a free man acquired a Raja's slave, he in turn was enslaved. According to the Pahang digest of 1596 if a man stole one of the Raja's slaves or killed one of the Raja's cattle, he had to restore fourteen-fold and if anyone disposed of a Raja's ornament or slave, he had to restore seven-fold. No one, it says, may resist a royal slave.

By becoming slaves of the Raja murderers could find sanctuary. In mediaeval Malacca only the Sultan could pardon a murderer, the abductor of a married woman and a person guilty of *lèse-majesté*. Only the Raja could behead without reference to any other authority. And without his authority no one might kill except he kill his wife's lover, a person guilty of *lèse-majesté*, a robber that defied capture or one guilty of such insult as slapping the face. Of all large fines the major portion went to the royal purse. So says the Malacca digest.

Mediaeval Malacca was the first kingdom in Malaya to see a great change in the title, lineage and duties of a ruler. Soon after A.D. 1400 Malacca embraced Islam. The old Sri Vijaya title, Sri Maharaja, was exchanged for Sultan. The Sultan though still entitled *sri paduka* was no longer an incarnate Hindu god but the shadow of Allah upon earth, and to compensate for this declension Muhammadan missionaries invented for Malay royalty a pedigree going back to that hero of Muslim folk-lore, Alexander the Great of the pseudo-Callisthenes. Muslim tracts taught the Malay sovereign that he was a servant of Allah and exhorted him to pursue justice and righteousness.

The constitution of this Muslim Malacca is the first in Malaya of which we have any adequate record.

A Malay ruler's heir was and is normally his eldest son, but preferably the son of a royal consort (*putra gahara*) or in old Malacca the son of a lady of the house of the Prime Ministers, cousins to the king. The eldest son was almost always fully royal, as the first consort of an important raja was always a lady of his own class. But to avoid disputes after his death a Malay ruler, like a Hindu king, nominated an Heir Apparent, the Raja Muda or Young Raja, during his life-time. In old Malacca the uxorious Sultan Mahmud changed his nomination three times, and following custom and the indication of his final choice his chiefs banished Muzaffar the son (by a Kelantan princess) who was Raja Muda and elected as Sultan his younger brother, son of a lady of the house of the Prime Ministers. In Perak, whose first Sultan that Muzaffar became, there sprang up early in the last century the practice of choosing rulers from three branches of the royal family in succession, a practice sometimes convenient as allowing latitude of choice and similar to the Minangkabau system for choosing tribal chiefs, as well as to the practice in some of the hereditary chieftainships in Perak. Fortified by this Minangkabau innovation, the Perak chiefs in 1871 just before British intervention refused to promote Raja Muda Abdullah to the throne because he was a cowardly cuckold and feared to attend his predecessor's obsequies as custom required. They also passed over another legitimist claimant as harsh and unpopular and appointed as Sultan a foreign Raja only related to Perak royalty by marriage. Under British administration one nominated heir was ousted in Pahang because to legitimist eyes the Sultan's choice was irregular and in Selangor a Raja Muda was deposed for conduct unbefitting high office. Clearly the choice of a Malay ruler by his chiefs was not a mere matter of form. And the exercise of this choice is still valuable, for experience has shown that chiefs are more likely to select a better candidate, than was a British official who was too often misled by a Cambridge School Certificate. In Perak the Raja Muda is the mouth-piece of the Sultan and is in charge of all the younger scions of the royal family.

In Malacca the title of the Heir Apparent was Sultan Muda or Young Sultan, and the style continued to be used in Perak down to the beginning of the present century. But in Perak the nature of the office became changed into that of state medicine-man and shaman. The duties the Sultan Muda then had to perform were to keep alive the weapons of the regalia, to conduct a feast for the royal drums, to sacrifice to the guardian genies of Perak and to be chief of all the shamans and medicine-men in the State. He was also court physician. According to one account he was too exalted to inherit any office but the Sultanate and according to another account he was ineligible even for that. On spear and distaff side he was expected to be of the royal house. His deputy and heir-apparent was styled Raja Kechil Muda. The last holder of the post of Sultan Muda was a *keramat* elder brother of Sultan Idris. For to-day the Perak state medicine-man is styled merely Pawang Raja. The dual Sultans in Perak apparently were a late innovation that may have been due to an accident in culture. Or the Perak state medicine-man may be a survival of some Hindu court magician or of the Purohita of Hindu days, the court chaplain who often from his education and intelligence usurped many of the functions of royalty. Malay historians invariably confine themselves to secular matters, so that evidence on the point is lacking.

The most important person near the old Malacca, Johor and Perak thrones was an officer who was at once prime minister and commander-in-chief. He bore the Indian title of Bendahara (? Skt. *Bhandagarika*), although he and other great commoner chiefs are sometimes addressed by a Sultan as *mamak*, a term commonly employed for a mother's eldest brother and family-head by Batak and Minangkabau. Significant, it would appear, of local as opposed to foreign Indian origin, was his duty of providing the ruler with a palace and with a daughter of his own house for consort; and a relic of the original bestowal of Malay thrones on foreigners may be the custom that, on the death of a Sultan, the Bendahara takes charge of the regalia and the baleful royal musical instruments and after seven days invites the heir to be installed. Alone of Malay chiefs the Bendahara could order executions not only in his own domain but anywhere in the State in the absence of the Sultan. He had jurisdiction over nobles and officials. And he was the leading figure at all court ceremonies and receptions. According to the Malacca digest whoever stabbed a buffalo belonging to the Bendahara or Temenggong or Major Chiefs or the Penghulu Bendahari or a Shahbandar became a debt-slave (*ulur*). According to the Pahang digest whoever killed the buffalo of a prince (other than the ruler) or of a Bendahara had to repay seven-fold; if the buffalo belonged to a Mantri, Sida-Sida or Bentara five-fold; if it belonged to common folk, two-fold. It was natural that the post of Bendahara, an office of such power, dignity and intimacy with the throne, should come in time in spite of being hereditary to be taken over by royalty as it has been in Perak, where since the 18th century the Bendahara has been a member of the royal house and ranks next to the Heir Apparent in succession to the throne. In modern Johor, too, the title is given to the Sultan's second son.

In an 18th century manuscript compiled for the Dutch Governor of Malacca, de Bruin, there is preserved a tradition that originally both the Bendahara and his heir the Temenggong (or Minister of Police) stood above the Four Major Chiefs or Mantri, and the *Sejarah Melayu* puts the Bendahari or Court Chamberlain also above the Four. If either of these statements is true, the earthly pattern of a heavenly kingdom was marred. In modern Perak the Four Privy Councillors (*Orang Empat di-balai*) consist of the Bendahara, the Orang Kaya Besar or Bendahari, the Temenggong and a Mantri Paduka Tuan.

In old Malacca, old Johor and old Perak the Temenggong ordinarily was of the same family as the Bendahara and succeeded to his office, though in Perak the passage of time has seen the post of Temenggong usurped by a family of Bugis adventurers. The Temenggong is unique among great chiefs to-day for an Indonesian title, found also in Majapahit, and everywhere his duties have always been the same, namely to build prisons, arrest criminals and carry out executions. When at night he went the rounds with the watch, he could kill any wayfarer not carrying a torch and anyone resisting arrest. In Perak he used to superintend forts and moats as well as prisons. In Perak as in Malacca he

F

supervised markets and weights and measures. Pires says he received dues on the merchandise. The title Temenggong has given its name to the Malay system of patriarchal law.

It is possible that the Bendahara represents a submerged indigenous chief, the equivalent of a proto-Malay Batin, and that the Temenggong was his assistant, the equivalent of the proto-Malay Jenang.

The Penghulu Bendahari (Hindustani *bhandari* from Skt. *bhandagarika*) belongs clearly to a later and more sophisticated period, when Indian influences had created port kingdoms and a literate court and the Hindustani of commerce had supplanted the earlier Sanskrit of the court. He was the ruler's chamberlain, secretary and treasurer. He dealt with the ruler's correspondence and had charge of the royal household. He kept a list of the ruler's slaves and collected the ruler's revenue, the Shahbandar or Port Officer coming under his department. In Malacca he was a member of the Bendahara family with the title Sri Nara 'diraja, and a Sri Nara 'diraja family furnished the earlier holders of the office in Perak until in the 18th century it was usurped by Sayids.

The Mantri Paduka Tuan in Perak was State Justiciar, holders being originally of the Malacca Bendahara family, then Sayids, then from a branch of the original family.

In Malacca there were Four Mantri of the first rank, Eight of middle rank and Sixteen of lower rank, the Thirty-Two not being entitled Mantri. According to the 18th century Malacca account, the Four bore the titles: Paduka Sri Ferdana Mantri, Paduka Maharaja, Paduka Maha Mantri and Paduka Sri Maharaja 'diraja.

Who ranked among the Eight in old Malacca is unknown. The 18th century account says that "any Mantri whose title began with Sri, for example, Sri Indra-wangsa, Sri Jaya Pahlawan, Sri Pekerma Raja, Sri Maharaja Lela,

Sri Raja 'diraja belonged to the Eight; sometimes also any Mantri whose title began with Paduka like Paduka Raja, or with Maha like Maharaja or with Raja like Raja Mahkota." Probably the titles and functions of the Perak Eight are a fair guide to those of their Malacca prototypes. At their head was a Maharaja Lela who at court ceremonies stood with drawn sword ready to behead on the spot and at his own discretion anyone guilty of a breach of loyalty or etiquette. There was the Admiral or Laksamana, whose title had sprung up in Malacca from a nickname taken from the Ramayana for a boy athlete. There was the important customs official, the Shahbandar or Port Officer. There was also the Imam Paduka Tuan, a Muslim religious dignitary. And the remaining four were territorial chiefs, all originally descendants of the Malacca Bendahara family and all bearing titles commonly found among old Malacca's territorial magnates: Sri Amara Wangsa 'diraja, Sri Amara 'diraja, Sri Agar 'diraja, Sri Nara 'diraja. In Pahang as in Malacca and Perak the Eight originally were hereditary.

That every Mantri had judicial functions is clear from the Malacca digest, which gives as their duties the collection of tribute (*ufti*), the investigation of truth, a knowledge of law, a fair hearing for both sides, and discretion in passing severe sentences. The same digest lays down the proportion of fines payable to the ruler, the Mandulikas and the Mantris. There was no divorce between the judicial and the executive.

The description Mandulika, a Sanskrit word meaning Governor, occurs on the 14th century Trengganu stele, in the Malacca and Pahang legal digests, in the "Malay Annals" as the former title of the territorial chief of Klang, and in the present titles of the Undang of Jelebu and of a Sungai Ujong chief. Tomé Pires tells us that there were Mandulikas at Cinyojum (Sungai Ujong), Klang, Selangor, Bernam, Mjmjam (? Manjong of the "Malay Annals"), Bruas and Perak. These Mandulikas had civil and criminal jurisdiction. They had to pay annual tribute to Malacca,

8000 *calains* of tin (which were worth double) for Mjmjam, 6000 each for Bruas and Selangor, 4000 each for Perak, Klang and Cinyojum. Their office may have dated back to Sri Vijaya, in view of its mention on the Trengganu stone.

In addition to general judicial functions, every Mantri must have had other duties. In Pahang before the British period the Four had authority to impose taxation and paid tribute to the ruler. The Maharaja Lela in Perak was a court official and territorial magnate. The Perak Laksamana held sway "up-river as far as the tide can reach, down-river to the line where the surf breaks on the bar and the grey mullet come to the surface." He had charge of the coast and it was his duty to guard against foreign foes and assist those in trouble at sea. He worked in concert with the Shahbandars and examined incoming and outgoing ships. The Shahbandars were harbour masters, customs' officers, protectors of immigrants and superintendents of trade. A Shahbandar's multifarious duties are set forth at greatest length in Kedah port laws of A.D. 1650 that recall similar regulations made by the Great Moguls. The Persian title of the office suggests that its foundation was due to overseas trade from India consequent on the coming of Muhammadanism. According to d'Albuquerque and Tomé Pires Malacca had four Shahbandars of different races, one and the most important for Gujeratis; one for Klings, Bengalis, Peguans and ships from Pasai; one for Malaysians; one for China, Indo-China and Luzon. Each man applied to the Shahbandar of his nation who presented him to the Bendahara, allotted him a warehouse, provided lodging and arranged for elephants.

According to the 18th century account of Malacca, the Four being distinguished by the exalted Paduka and the Eight by the honorific Sri, all that was left for the Sixteen was Raja, and it gives as examples Raja Awadana Lela, Raja Stia Pahlawan, Raja Dewa Pahlawan, Raja Putra Jaya, Raja Putra Indra, Raja Derma Indra, Raja Utama Stia. Kedah also differentiated at least in theory between the grades Paduka, Sri and Raja. In Perak if Raja ever was the generic style for the Sixteen, it has no longer survived, except for a Raja Mahkota, and the Sixteen include two Padukas, five Sris and three Maharajas. In Pahang the Sixteen were styled To' Muda.

In Perak the Sixteen minor chiefs were mostly cadets of the families of the Four Great and Eight Major Chiefs. Royal favour or dislike and the character and intelligence of individual chiefs must have often created or annulled lesser titles and raised and lowered the precedence of lesser offices. In Pahang the Sixteen were appointed by the Major Chiefs of the district, and office was not hereditary.

Below these, in theory at least, Malacca and Perak had the Thirty-Two, who unlike the superior classes of chief were not ministers (*manteri*) but most of them minor assistants of the greater chiefs or else territorial headmen of small areas.

Clearly both in old Malacca and in more modern Perak the council of Great and Lesser Chiefs developed to meet changing conditions. In Malacca the inner cabinet was for a while composed of members of the greatest commoner family, that of the Bendaharas, and it was this family that chose Sultans and conducted home and foreign policy, often corruptly and with an eye to self-interest. The main task of Malacca's ministers was to direct an imperialist policy for the advancement of the royal dynasty and the expansion of a trade, that brought wealth to the Ruler and to themselves in the shape of taxes and presents. Above have been given the annual sums paid by the Mandulikas and according to Tomé Pires, Kampar, Indragiri and Pahang each paid the Sultan of Malacca 4 katis (or 5⅓ lbs.) of gold a year.

As for home policy, both in Malacca and in modern Malay States, there was no expenditure on roads or education or on any of the ends of a modern civilised government. Instead of a regular army there were only a collection of swashbucklers and Indian mercenaries, attached to the court or to the households of the greater chiefs. Justice was not reformative but savage and deterrent. The only civil servants were police and tax-collectors. Taxes before the British period were framed to extort revenue to enhance the wealth and importance of ruler and chiefs. In 1786 Francis Light wrote how the Sultan of Kedah got his income from monopolies, presents and fines; he also levied a small duty upon every plough and upon the sale of cattle and slaves. In 19th-century Perak the Sultan got his income from large fines and from duties not only on tin, opium and tobacco, but on rattans, hides, gums, salt-fish and oil; the Heir Apparent's income came from gambling houses, opium saloons and spirit shops; the Bendahara enjoyed tolls on goods carried up and down the Kinta river and a capitation tax of 50 cents from every household collected, be it noted, by the musicians of the royal band; the Temenggong enjoyed a monopoly of the sale of salt and ataps, fees on weights and court fines and river tolls. The Sri Adika Raja, a territorial chief, enjoyed fines, certain fees, royalties on tin and gutta-percha, and annual tribute of 70 *gantang* of rice from every household in his area. The Panglima Kinta enjoyed fines, fees and a royalty of 10 per cent. on all Kinta tin. In 1874 Perak export duties were: $6 to $10 on a *bahar* (400 lbs.) of tin, $3 a *pikul* (133⅓ lbs.) on gutta-percha, $2 a *pikul* on resin, $1.25 a *pikul* on hides, $2 on a 100 rattans. There were numerous import duties: $4 a *koyan* (or 1000 gallons) on rice, $50 on a chest of opium, $16 a *koyan* on salt, $2 a *pikul* on Javanese and $1.50 a *pikul* on Chinese tobacco; 2½ per cent. *ad valorem* on cottons and silks. At every rivermouth the local chief had a customs station, and duties were demanded at every station past which goods were conveyed. Even "Eyes", the contemporary policeman, got his tithe of poultry, rope, pots and pans, needles, gold and silk thread, coconuts and fish and demanded $2 a mast from vessels passing his coign of vantage. In every Malay State there was the same licensed extortion. Even in democratic Negri Sembilan the four Undang enjoyed fines, levies, a poll-tax of $4 to $6 a head on imported slaves (that cost $20 to $60 each) and the forced labour of their subjects.

POLITICAL SYSTEMS 79

Royalties had to be paid to Negri Sembilan chiefs on the produce of tin mines and gold mines, and sometimes the chiefs retained the right to purchase a certain percentage of the metal below market price. Nor was it only the holders of state offices that exacted tax and toll in a Malay country. Many members of the prolific royal families claimed the right to collect taxes on river tributaries.

The only departments of government from which the peasant derived any benefit for himself were the departments of religion and magic, but for those benefits he had to contribute. "Muslims," it is said in Perak's 18th-century digest, the Ninety-Nine Laws, "must feed the district judge, the officers of the mosque, the medicine-men and the midwife. The muezzin is king in the mosque, and the medicine-man is king in the house of the sick, in the rice-field and the mine. A parish medicine-man must be long-headed, suave, industrious and truthful, and he must not have intrigues with women-folk. If a person is sick, he must attend immediately. His reward is that he escapes taxation and forced labour." Again, "A medicine-man's fee for taking care (*bela*) of a village is a gold *paha* and the remains of the feast; for taking care of a mine and its spirits, he gets the same plus a black jacket and headkerchief. Medicinemen vivify whatever has been damaged and their fee for doing this on a hill-clearing or elsewhere is a length of white cloth and the remains of the feast; once every three months a magician vivifies the rice-plants, so as to earn his fee of two *derham* from each cultivator."

The best feature of this mediaeval government was that ordinarily the Sultan did consult his chiefs over important matters. In all treaties between Malay Rulers and the Dutch and English there appear after the seal of the Sultan the seals of major chiefs.

In modern Johor and modern Pahang, where in the last century the Temenggong, local representative in Johor of the Riau-Johor-Pahang empire, and the Bendahara, local representative of that same empire in Pahang, assumed both of them the style of Sultans, the political constitutions of to-day are a mixture of old and new. In Pahang the old Malacca constitution has been copied with Minangkabau accretions. In Johor the new Sultan created three councils modelled on the Privy Council of Great Britain, and the Executive and Legislative Councils of British colonies. In the new Federation every State now has an Executive and Legislative Council.

The constitutions of Selangor, Kedah, Kelantan and Trengganu have never been adequately studied. Kedah appears to have been influenced by subjugation to Acheh more than Perak, where only a few titles and the classification of the Eight as Hulubalang or territorial chiefs betray Achinese interference.

The two basic principles of the Malay patriarchal system, the consultation of chiefs by the ruler and administration of districts through territorial magnates, made easy the introduction of State Councils and administration of the parish by a Malay Penghulu (or headman) and of districts at first by British officers and, as time passed, by more and more Malay officers. A Commissioner of Police was the counterpart of the Temenggong. A Commissioner of Customs and his department took the place of the Shahbandar and his underlings. There was in fact no radical change in machinery. But the Sultans were persuaded to appoint British and Chinese members to their Councils. And there was now established a central authority against which a forest-clad country with no roads or railways had always imposed insuperable barriers. Even the old Malacca digest had had constantly to reiterate the penalties for those who took the law into their own hands, often to the extent of executing without obtaining the sanction of the Ruler. Under Malay rule, too, not even the justice of the central authority was fixed and unalterable, but it would vary according to the age and disposition of the Sultan and the suppleness of his advisers. One reign and even one district

A Kedah Market

would see the mild old-world indigenous system of compensation in force; while a new Ruler or a neighbouring chief would prefer some harsh provision of Hindu or Muslim law. Under the British, justice, though often harsh, became everywhere uniform and always honest. The institution of a central authority also brought one system of taxation and ensured that a trader would no longer be called upon to pay tax and toll on the same cargo at the estuary of every tributary of a State's main river. Moreover not only was taxation thus reformed but revenue was expended for the good of the people as well as for the aggrandizement of their chiefs.

Mistakes, of course, occurred in the beginning of British administration. Mr. Birch, the first Resident of Perak, was murdered because he failed to discover chiefs had no arbitrary power to introduce innovations that traversed established custom. Custom knew all about slavery and nothing about all men being by nature free and equal in the sight of the law. Custom took time to discover that the killing of a witch or werewolf was murder. People who had always planted rice on dry hill-clearings knew nothing of the objectives of forestry and at first hated the burden of ploughing and weeding wet rice fields. Whereas judgments and regulations ordained in accordance with tradition were regarded as part of the natural order, inevitably the powers of chiefs paid by the British government came to be bureaucratic and were sometimes misunderstood and resented. In the old world, headmen had been chosen for their personality, their address, enterprise, courage and humanity; in the new, they were sometimes appointed because they were competent at arithmetic, and they were sometimes transferred to a *mukim* where they were utter strangers.

II Matrilineal

Whereas the Malay patriarchal system underwent strong foreign influence from the top downwards, the matrilineal system of Negri Sembilan grew up from the family, with royalty as little more than an ornamental accretion. Study therefore can best proceed from the *mamak* or mother's eldest brother, the head of her family, through the elder of the sub-tribe, the head of the tribe and the territorial chief up to the Yang di-pertuan or Yamtuan, supreme arbiter in constitutional and judicial questions between the territories.

Leaving aside those purely family heads, one's "wife's relations", the lowest rung on the political ladder is filled by the elder of the sub-tribe.

The Elder (Buapa)

Every sub-tribe (*perut*) has according to its size one or more elders (*buapa*), elected by its members and approved by the tribal chief, who can dismiss them at will. The tribal chief is described in tribal sayings as a hawk but the elder rather irreverently as a chattering mynah bird whose province is not tribal lands like that of the tribal chief but the disputatious tribal folk. Whereas no one may slaughter a buffalo without inviting the tribal chief, no one may slaughter a goat without inviting the elder. When an elder dies, he is entitled like all his betters to a coffin of betel-palm, whereas the ordinary person has a coffin of bamboo! Every elder must be aware of the family relationships, the extra-tribal acquisitions and payments, the quarrels and misdeeds of the members of his sub-tribe. While the tribal chief is expressly concerned with tribal lands, the elder is the proper qualified witness for all formal payments made to or by a member of the sub-tribe, the declaration of a husband's private property at marriage and its return at divorce. Before the days of British protection he, like the tribal and territorial chiefs and the Yam-tuan, had his own defined jurisdiction in civil and criminal cases. To-day he sanctions the mildest form of irregular marriage and reports to the tribal chief more serious forms. Failure to report offences beyond his jurisdiction makes him a traitor to the tribal chief and renders him liable to dismissal. Under the constitution the tribal chief appointed a magnate (*besar*) to spy on his elders, just as the territorial chief appointed a magnate to spy on him! This system of spies may have been introduced with Hinduism from India where it was common. It was due to Minangkabau influence that the Sultan of Pahang also has these magnates, termed in Pahang Orang Besar Raja.

The Tribal Chief (Lembaga)

When fresh tribal land was acquired, it was the tribal chief who in Malay days marked the boundaries, after the territorial chief (or Undang) had fixed the price. When the property of a tribeswoman changes hands on death or by sale, it is he who still attends at the Collector's office to guard the interests of his tribe. He is concerned with all offences that may damage his tribe's interests, whether they are the crimes, torts or debts of an individual or the misdeeds of an elder or of a territorial chief.

The tribal chief, like the territorial, must never die. If an election cannot be settled before the burial of a deceased Lembaga, then the elder of the deceased's sub-tribe acts temporarily. Often fights at the grave side and indecent delay of the obsequies occurred.

Each of the fully enfranchised sub-tribes should in turn provide a holder for the office, though if the sub-tribe whose turn it is cannot furnish a suitable candidate, it loses that turn. When a Lembaga dies, if his sub-tribe fails to bury him with due ceremony, it loses for ever the right to have any of its members appointed to the office.

A tribal chief is elected by the elders of the sub-tribe, supported by the fully enfranchised members of the tribe, male and female, and by its lesser headmen, and he can be removed only by their unanimous vote. He must be dismissed if he harbours or abets an offender, if he causes wrongful gain or loss to one of his tribe, if he brings shame on the tribe or if he is caught in an illicit love affair. An old friend of mine, who had been elected in spite of having an "unlucky" cross-eye, nearly lost office because he was so undignified as to drive his own bullock-cart. A tribal chief may also be dismissed for open opposition to the territorial chief. It at the election of a new Lembaga the electors fail to reach unanimity, the choice is made by the territorial chief in council with the other tribal chiefs. No election or dismissal is valid until confirmed by the territorial chief. If the council of the territorial chief cannot agree, then the matter goes now to the State Council for the Yam-tuan and the four territorial chiefs formerly with the British Resident to "disentangle the intricate, clear the turbid and disperse the mist". If a tribal chief is going away for a short period, say, to make the pilgrimage to Mecca, he may suggest some one, usually the elder of his own sub-tribe, to act for him, but his nominee must still be approved by the electors and the territorial chief. Old age or illness may compel him to summon the electors and tender his resignation in set phrases:—"The valleys have grown too deep for my going, the hills too steep for my climbing and journeys too far for my feet. Burdens have become too heavy for my back and light tasks for my fingers." The procedure for election is the same as in the other cases.

Elected, a Lembaga invites the tribe to a public feast called "the sprinkling of the broken grain" for all the denizens of the village, "the cocks that lay not eggs, the hens that cackle and the chickens that chirp". He sprinkles the grain as a symbol of gathering them under his wing and the bond of tribal unity is acknowledged in old-world sentences:—

> Together we skin the elephant's liver,
> Together dip the liver of the louse;
> What we drop is common loss;
> What we gain is common profit.[1]

The Territorial Chief (Undang)

The Minangkabau colonists of Negri Sembilan did not bring territorial chiefs from their homeland. Others were already in possession, whom they gradually merged into

[1] See Appendix A, p. 184.

their matrilineal system and termed Undang or Lawgivers. Dato' Klana Putra, Undang of Sungai Ujong, represents a chieftainship, that as far back as the 14th century was created by the first Sultan of Malacca and, becoming Bugis, even in the 18th century was inherited by patrilineal descent. The Undangs of Rembau and Johol claim descent from Bendahara Sekudai, a Johor descendant of those same Malacca viziers. The early Malacca-sprung chiefs convinced the Minangkabau newcomers of their title to the soil—explaining, as soon as they grasped the principles of mother right, that their title was got by inter-marriage with aboriginal women! Johol, Jelebu and Sungai Ujong still humour the aborigines by pretending to regard them as owners of the soil.

The method of electing the territorial chiefs is significant as showing how far Minangkabau custom penetrated inland. In Rembau and Naning the tribal chiefs elect by their unanimous vote the territorial chiefs from different uterine sub-tribes, offshoots of the original patriarchal Malacca house (p. 58). In Jelebu the Undang is elected by a Council of eight, of whom five represent the Malacca *waris* family and only three are Lembaga, representing Minangkabau tribes. In Johol, Baginda Tan Mas, head of the *waris* is elected to his office by the Jenang (a Malay chief with an aboriginal title) and the six elders of the non-Minangkabau Biduanda tribe, and on a vacancy he becomes now automatically Undang. In Sungai Ujong the Undang is elected by the elders of the two Malacca-sprung *waris* families, eligible for the post, or failing their unanimous vote by four minor *territorial* chiefs who are now improperly styled Lembaga.

Every Undang is head of the *waris* family, whose inheritance comprises all the land in the State not alienated to the Minangkabau settlers, all "the ravines and valleys, hills and gorges and tree-cumbered jungle paths". As head he is allotted the lion's share of the revenue from these sources. In Rembau he used to get tribute of parched and husked rice from all squatters on unalienated land together with a duty on minerals and agricultural produce exported by miners and foreign planters. These sources of revenue have been mostly commuted now for fixed allowances to members of the *waris* families, while in Rembau so great have been the profits from rubber lands that in addition to these allowances a *waris* fund has been started for the erection of mosques and public works of utility to the Malays. Unlike the Yam-tuan, the Undangs were rich.

An Undang, however, is a commoner:—in theory, the smallest raja ranks as high as an Undang. But they were (and are) independent:—they collaborated in the face of Bugis invaders and then fell apart. When, however, they came together under British protection, the Dato' Klana of Sungai Ujong, the chief of oldest descent, whose ancestor is reputed to have summoned the first Yam-tuan, was once more their spokesman. Unless any of them desired to refer a matter to the Yam-tuan (which in practice never happened), the Undang sitting in council with the tribal or tribal and *waris* chiefs interpreted custom and had powers of execution with the creese.

The state maintained by an Undang is considerable. His appropriate number is 5 against 3 for the tribal chief and 7 for the Yam-tuan:—a salute of 5 guns, a wedding lasting 5 days, a dais of 5 storeys and a bier of 5 storeys. His insignia include flags, umbrellas, weapons, canopies, curtains, a tent on his lawn and a gong to announce his movements. When the Undang of Jelebu is buried, nine maidens stand on the litter, eight keeping the corpse in position with their extended hands, while the ninth holds aloft a young plantain-tree as a symbol that the office never dies.

The Ruler (Yang Di-pertuan)

For a long time the Minangkabau settlers were content to be under the protection of whatever neighbouring power could secure them peace, their territorial Malacca-descended chiefs gradually adopting Minangkabau custom but being careful to get recognition from the Dutch in Malacca and from the Sultans of Johor. In the 18th century the murder of a Sultan of Johor dragged them into conflict with the heir and his supporters, the Bugis of Riau. So they sent for a Minangkabau prince to defend them and at last found a paladin in a Raja Melewar, whom they created Yang di-pertuan or, to use the colloquial, Yam-tuan.

Though the first Yam-tuan "strengthened the succession by humouring matrilineal ideas" and marrying a daughter of the first Chief of Muar, yet the royal family could and afterwards did marry within itself: cousins for example, the children of brothers, have commonly married. The second and third Yam-tuans were *husbands of the daughter and grand-daughter* of Raja Melewar. Since then succession has gone through the male line. But the office does not descend by primogeniture. The Yam-tuan is elected by the four territorial chiefs—formally to-day, though in the past there were disputes, some claiming that the Yamtuan should always be a delegate from Minangkabau, others that his mother as well as his father must be royal or else of the tribe of the Muar wife of Raja Melewar.

The appointment was after the model of the Minangkabau constitution. Like the Raja of the Minangkabau world at Pagar Ruyong, the Yam-tuan was supreme arbiter, the final court of appeal. Perhaps among the Yam-tuan's insignia the ring and the hair (which Karens and Malays use for divination) are relics of the early days of this royal justiciar. Minangkabau sayings define his position:—

> The Raja is the fount of equity,
> The Chief carries out the law,
> The cord for arrest is the tribal headman's,
> The execution creese is the territorial chief's,
> The headman's sword is the Raja's—
> He can stab without asking leave of any suzerain,
> He can behead without reporting it to any suzerain.[1]

[1] See Appendix A, p. 184.

In a matrilineal community he had these rights of a patriarchal king—if the matrilineal territorial chiefs allowed appeal to him! Like the Raja at Pagar Ruyong, the Yam-tuan owns no state territory:—as a Jelebu customary saying cynically remarks, "the highroads with their stepping-stones belong to the prince and the bulbuls!" Nor can the Yam-tuan levy taxes: any attempt to do so would cause him to be cast out "upon a waveless sea and a grassless field", or in plain language to be expelled. Actually he lived on the land acquired through Raja Melewar's tribal commoner wife; on offerings of money, rice and coconuts, made at his accession and at circumcision and marriage feasts; and, in the old days, on fees for cock-fights. He was Caliph, head of the Muslim Faith—in any territory where the local chief did not proclaim himself Caliph! In short, the only one of his attributes that one or other of the territorial chiefs has not claimed from time to time is his immemorial sanctity as a white-blooded prince. He was allowed the usual ceremonial rights of Malay rulers, namely, the right of using and of permitting others to use weapons sheathed in gold or silver and styles of architecture confined to sovereigns. Tabu to all but royalty were yellow clothes; skirts all black, white or red; a silk cummerbund fastening the skirt with the creese thrust through it; the wearing of a scarf over the shoulder; divan mats adorned with gold or silver; be-jewelled head-cloths and modesty-pieces for children made of coconut-shell! Tabu were the styles of tying the head-dress called "The Chief returns from bathing" and "Split-ting the young coconut", also the tying of it with all four ends projecting. And it was tabu to enter the palace precincts using an umbrella or carrying a scarf or betel-set suspended from the shoulder. The violator of any of these tabus could be fined 24 dollars. For like other Malay rulers the Yam-tuan of Negri Sembilan was descended from kings who had been incarnations of Hindu deities, and, as we have seen, he was the inheritor of astrological superstitions.

"At every stage," Lord Simon once said, "the British

constitution has developed by making a new brick, placing a new step, removing some definite concrete obstacle." The Negri Sembilan constitution developed on similar lines though it failed until the days of British protection to remove two concrete obstacles to its perfection. It dealt skilfully with patrilineal intruders, the pre-Minangkabau inhabitants, and the later aliens from Malacca and Acheen, allotting to them tribes and tribal chiefs and absorbing them into its comity. It dealt skilfully with those who claimed the country under gift from the patriarchal Sultans of Malacca and their successors the patriarchal Sultans of Johor: they became territorial chiefs, but chiefs who soon discarded patriarchal custom for Minangkabau mother-right. The legal system was adaptable, jurisdiction was well graded and in theory there was a supreme arbiter, the Yam-tuan, above State prejudices, with comparative data and final jurisdiction. "In itself," wrote Mr. R. J. Wilkinson very justly, "the gradation of official powers is no protection of the liberty of the subject. Its effectiveness in Negri Sembilan lay in the fact that the higher authorities were like our own appellate or assize courts: they could not initiate an attack on an individual. If the peasant committed a petty offence, he was judged by his own people: the chief could not interfere. If he was charged with a graver crime, he was heard by his own people and if a *prima facie* case was made out against him, he was handed over to the higher authorities for trial. . . . The (territorial) chief could not proceed against any one except the tribal headman, nor was he strong enough to attack any single Lembaga unjustly in face of the opposition that such a proceeding would arouse among the rest." In spite of the good points of this constitution there were two imperfections that were never mended. First of all there was the basic Minangkabau principle that for every election and every decision complete unanimity is required:—

> As a bamboo conduit makes a round jet of water,
> So taking counsel together rounds men to one mind.[1]

Unanimity is obviously a survival from early days of family

[1] See Appendix A. p. 184.

rule, but though they have long since outgrown family rule, the Minangkabaus have never learnt to bow to the decision of the majority: until the British came, minorities always broke away and created civil strife. Secondly there was the anomalous position of the Yam-tuan. These simple frugal democratic villagers failed to recognize that to be incorruptible even an arbiter must be set above want, and have an adequate privy purse. Moreover to enforce his decrees he must have power, a point they saw and reasonably feared. The old Nine States never were a homogeneous Minangkabau federation. The big territorial chiefs who professed the matrilineal system in its entirety never merged their individual interests in those of the federation, as tribes through the need for inter-marriage had merged theirs from time immemorial. Except in the face of a foreign aggressor each State was self-sufficient, so that until the days of British protection the territorial chiefs never met regularly in council with the Yam-tuan as each one of them met in council with his own tribal chiefs. The British creation of a Council for the Nine States of which the Yam-tuan is president and the Undangs are members put the coping-stone on the Negri Sembilan constitution.

6: LEGAL SYSTEMS

OUR knowledge of Malay legal systems is based partly on digests of law, partly on tribal sayings and partly on the evidence elicited in modern suits to determine inheritance and the division of property.

The digests of law collected from all the races of the Malay archipelago fill many large printed volumes. In the Malay peninsula they are of four main types:—

(1) There are digests and tribal sayings that embody the mild indigenous matriarchal law of agricultural clans, the *'adat perpateh* or law of Ministers, cherished by the Minangkabaus of Sumatra and their colonists in Negri Sembilan.

(2) There are digests, containing traces of Malay indigenous patriarchal law, but mixed with relics of Hindu law and overlaid with Muslim law. This patriarchal law is called *'adat Temenggong* or law of the Minister for War and Police. Evolved for the mixed population of ports, it was introduced largely from India along with commerce by traders and adventurers, at first Hindu and later Muslim. For our knowledge of this composite patriarchal law we are indebted especially to the Malacca digest of c. 1450 A.D., the Pahang digest of 1596 with a later supplement, and to a Kedah digest dated 1650 and containing port rules adopted by countries like Acheh and Kedah from regulations of the kind India knew from the days of Chandra Gupta and embodied in the Mogul *Tarikh-i-Tahiri*. Even the 18th century Ninety-Nine Laws of Perak belong to this composite class, although compiled by Sayids and exhibiting Shi'ite influence. The Johor digest is mainly based on that of Malacca, and in a M.S. known to de Hollander is dated "about 1789".

(3) There are digests of maritime law, the earliest compiled for the last Sultan of Malacca in consultation with sea-captains for Bugis and Macassar trading-ships.

(4) Lastly, there are Malay translations of orthodox Muslim works of the school of Shafi'i, especially treatises on the law of marriage, divorce and the legitimacy of children, the only branch of Muslim canon law that Malays have adopted practically unchanged.

On the Malay principle of "reading from *alif* and counting from one", we shall best illustrate the historical evolution of Malay law by starting with the indigenous matrilineal law of the Minangkabau colonists of Negri Sembilan.

I Matrilineal Law

Only comparison with the despotic law of the other states of Malaya can explain why in Negri Sembilan the matrilineal customary law lived as a *magna carta* in the hearts and memories of the Minangkabaus it had saved for centuries from oppression. "A couch to the sleeper, a shelter to the wayfarer, a ship to the navigator, an ancestral estate to the cultivator, a true measure that neither damp can mildew nor heat warp." That is how, in one of their many picturesque tribal sayings, they extol a legal system that had universal and constant validity.

Cynics might complain that this matrilineal custom changed with every new chief, as landing-places shift with the tide, that in Rembau it was twisted and knotty and in Jelebu turned round about like a water-wheel; but despite these grumblings and despite modifications admitted to allow it to keep pace with the times, there was never any radical change in its principles. No Raja dared to violate them, for fear of being "cast out on a waveless sea or a grassless plain", or in blunt words, of being dethroned and stranded. No Kadli could win acceptance if he attempted to annul one line of this custom's unorthodox provisions. Its administration was subject to the firmest democratic controls of an agricultural community, whose circumstances remained unchanged down the centuries with no foreign trade and no foreign settlers to alter and widen them. Every Minangkabau peasant knew by heart and understood the sayings that embodied his tribal law, and the clever wove them into endless digests that essayed the impossible task of reconciling the rules of exogamous clans with the Muslim canon.

Now life in a clan is communal, so that the death penalty, imprisonment and mutilation involved the loss of a pair of hands to the tribe. Hence the Minangkabau punishment for crime, except in the case of heinous and incorrigible offenders, always took the form of restitution. If a man wounded in an assault lost a little blood, his assailant gave him a fowl, if a lot of blood, a goat. The cooked flesh was presented to the wounded man. His assailant took him to a stream or well, anointed his head with the blood of the fowl or goat, then with rice and finally with juice of lime to cleanse away the blood and rice. If a tribesman were killed, the chief of his tribe chose a substitute of the same sex from the tribe of the slayer, or, if slayer and slain were of the same tribe, the slayer's family had to pay a fine of one buffalo and fifty bushels of husked rice. The territorial chief might, further, sentence a slayer to be creesed or outlawed, but this was perhaps a Malaccan accretion on the Minangkabau system.

The weakest point in this customary law was its undue reliance on circumstantial evidence:—

> Customary law requires signs of guilt;
> Religious law calls for witnesses.
> When customary law meets circumstances obscure,
> It throws wide its net. . . .
> Crime leaves its trail like a water-beetle;
> Like a snail, it leaves its slime;
> Like a horse-mango, it leaves its reek;
> A stream that knows not its source or its mouth,
> Like that is a man who cannot account for his doings;
> Where a dog barks is where the iguana climbs.[1]

[1] See Appendix, p. 184.

Minangkabau law employed a "ladder" to inspect "the broken branch", a "ladle" to "catch the dew" on the criminal's garments, a "cast-net" to enmesh the fleeing thief. The production of a piece of a man's trousers by an unwedded mother was enough to prove the paternity of a child.

This flaw in the Minangkabau system was to a large extent remedied by jurisdiction being independent of the arbitrary whim of hereditary ruler or territorial chief; seeing, that, in tribal phrase, "pots are for cooking and mortars for pounding", it was clearly defined. The elected elder of the sub-tribe tried cases of assault involving a wound or a broken skin, provided the scar was on a part of the body concealed by clothing. Assault involving permanent disfigurement, cases of grievous hurt involving loss of sight, broken bones and ruptured sinews, these came before the higher court of the elected tribal chief. Then there was a list of capital crimes, that were accounted offences not against the tribe but against the state, such as treason, arson, robbery, theft, tribal incest, cheating, poisoning and stabbing. In origin they must have been tribal offences and not offences against a state that came into being later. Incest, for example, meant marriage to a woman of one's own tribe, namely a marriage that brought no new worker and no new property to the tribe. But all these capital offences had come to be reserved for trial before the Undang or territorial chief, who was originally a lord lieutenant appointed by the Sultans of 15th century Malacca, but later was assimilated to the Minangkabau constitution and elected.

British advice set aside Minangkabau customary law in criminal cases. The British law of evidence is stricter and more favourable to an accused person. The British would not recognize as incest marriage to a remote tribal relative or treat as criminal a man's liaison with a woman of the same tribe as his wife. Where accident was proved, it would not convict of homicide. What was cheating under Minangkabau custom was sometimes a civil offence under English law. But the compounding of serious crime was

LEGAL SYSTEMS

forbidden. Robbery and theft, arson, homicide, criminal breach of trust and obtaining money by false pretences were tried under the Indian Penal Code, which cares nothing for tribal loss or for compensation in the shape of fowls, goats and sisters' sons.

Yet if criminal law in Negri Sembilan became British, the law of property remained matrilineal, and hardly affected even by the Muslim canon. Ancestral property (*harta pusaka*) devolves from mothers to daughters or to their direct female descendants. If a daughter has died whose share of her mother's or aunt's property would have been one half, her two daughters get a quarter each, or if there are three of them, a sixth each. As among the Khassis, the mother's house is ordinarily inherited by the youngest daughter who undertakes in return to look after her in her old age. Her sisters must help her to keep this house in repair and she cannot sell or charge it without their approval. Failing direct heirs, a woman's ancestral property goes to her sisters and her sisters' daughters and grand-daughters and even to great-great-grand-daughters. But if the nearest female relatives are cousins removed beyond the fourth degree, the property may be sold and the proceeds paid to male heirs in default of female heirs of the same degree. Moreover now in most of the states male heirs may claim life-tenancy of ancestral lands—for example, in the absence of daughters a son may claim, or in the absence of grand-daughters grandsons may claim.

Other items of ancestral property are prized weapons, ornaments and clothing. Some of these heirlooms are used by the men, but their title to that use comes through mothers and sisters. A man comes into possession of creese or spear through his mother. On his death the weapon goes not to his son (who is not of his father's tribe) but back to his mother for the use of her next son, or back to his sister for the use of her eldest son, or, if his sister is dead, to his niece, her daughter, for the use of the niece's eldest son or eldest brother.

A distinction is drawn between a woman's ancestral property, of which her tribe has no usufruct but almost absolute control, and her personal property of which while alive she has usufruct and absolute control, though after the original owner's death it has been apt normally to become at any rate in the third generation ancestral.

> Stretches of rice-field,
> Paths over the knolls in the swamps,
> Old betel-nut palms,
> Ancestral coconut-palms
> Belong to the tribal chief.[1]

This saying is important as it enunciates the theory that ancestral property belongs to the tribe rather than to any individual tribeswoman. Another saying shows what action is still taken if the woman holder (who is clearly no more than her tribe's trustee for her lifetime) tries to dispose of ancestral property by sale or to charge it.

> Her next-of-kin can approve or prevent;
> If there are heiresses or heirs, they can find the money,
> And subscribe to save the tail;
> If there are next-of-kin, they can bar the sale;
> If the property has an owner, the sale is quashed;
> If there is a tribal headman, he can quash it.[2]

It looks as if formerly, so long as there was a member of the tribe left, sale outside the tribe was forbidden. To-day only to meet certain customary debts it may be allowed. But the next-of-kin, that is, children and grand-children, can still bar sale or charge; while indirect collateral heiresses, though they cannot bar them if the direct heiresses consent, yet have the option of purchase or of lending the sum required and taking the land as security. Custom allows this pre-emption, first to relatives in order of matrilineal nearness, failing them to members of the sub-tribe and failing them to members, female or even male, of the tribe. Rather than let the land be lost to the tribe, its chief will

[1]See Appendix A, p. 184.
[2]See Appendix A, p. 185.

do his best to persuade the vendor to take a lower price from a member of her own tribe than she could get in the open market. The only person to whom a land-owner can convey ancestral land by gift to the detriment of natural heiresses is a woman whom she has fully adopted into her tribe, but this creates no departure from the principle: once tribal land, always tribal land.

What obligations have these women land-owners towards their men-folk? They had, in former times, to pay compensation for a brother's misdeeds and crimes so as to prevent the offender and themselves becoming debt-slaves. Do they have to pay for gambling debts and his speculations in tin and rubber? At least once a British judge misconstrued the custom and held them liable. Actually a Minangkabau man can bind only himself so far as his personal acquired property, the fruit of his own industry and saving, is concerned. If his creditor is not satisfied with that security, he must arrange for the debt to be guaranteed by the head of the man's family after agreement by all its members.

A tribesman or tribeswoman may have separate property that is not ancestral of which a married pair have usufruct in common. A man may have separate property (*harta pembawa*) acquired by his bachelor savings or inherited from a previous wife or given him by his parents. A woman may have separate property (*harta dapatan*) acquired by her as spinster, divorcée or widow. Such property reverts on death to the tribal heirs of the deceased, namely to his or her nearest female relatives. On divorce, it goes back to the husband or the wife, whoever owned it originally, that is, it remains within his or her tribe, but any increase in the value of the man's separate property may be divided equally between the man and the woman.

For all property acquired during married life (*harta charian laki bini*) is, on divorce, divided equally. To this general rule there are two exceptions. The husband may grant his half or part of it to the issue of the marriage. And if the marriage has been subject to a condition (*nikah ta'alik*) that, should the husband be absent six months ashore or a year overseas without communicating with his wife, divorce takes place automatically, then the woman retains the whole of the property acquired during the broken marriage.

On death property acquired during a childless marriage devolves on the surviving spouse. If the husband leaves issue, it goes to his widow with remainder to the issue of the marriage. If the wife dies leaving issue, it may be divided equally between the widower and the issue or in such proportions as the two families and the tribal chiefs decide. Practice still differs in the several districts. In Jelebu property acquired during marriage still devolves even at the death of its first joint owner according to the matrilineal system. In Rembau since 1930 there have been isolated cases of the distribution of such property to heirs of both sexes in accordance with the fractional shares prescribed by Muhammadan law. In Kuala Pilah court influence has led to the observance of the Muslim law of succession in a number of cases. In 1929 a competent British authority, Mr. Justice A. N. Taylor, wrote expressing the view that the tribes desired the continuance of tribal restrictions on ancestral land (*tanah pusaka*) and on the separate personal property of husband (*harta pembawa*) and wife (*harta dapatan*), but they favour freedom of transfer for property newly acquired (*harta charian*). As for the devolution of land jointly acquired during marriage (*harta charian laki bini*), it is generally desired that sons as well as daughters shall inherit and that, especially if the marriage has been childless, a surviving husband shall inherit. Having these views in mind, Mr. Taylor suggested certain general principles for the guidance of officials concerned:—

(a) If a marriage is childless, property acquired during it should devolve on the surviving spouse.

(b) If there is issue of a marriage, then such property devolves on the widow with remainder to that issue. Or if the wife dies, it is divided between the widower and the issue of the marriage, provided that, should the widower get no support from his own tribe, then such property devolves on him with remainder to the issue of the marriage. Before acquired property is distributed, funeral expenses and debts have to be defrayed out of it.

It cannot be claimed that the British administered the matrilineal law of succession to property in an informed manner or framed appropriate legislation to carry it into effect. A basic error was the failure to recognize that the law follows not the land but the person. Collectors transferred from other states were swayed by a bias towards the Muslim law of succession, with which they were already acquainted, in preference to the intricacies of a matrilineal law of which they were ignorant. Judges failed to distinguish between the various classes of personal property or, contemptuous of the unwritten, based erroneous decisions on such European anachronisms as the entry of the word "Customary" on a title.

II Patriarchal Law

The Malacca digest gives the earliest picture of Malay patriarchal law. For although copyists have interpolated references to Mahmud, last Sultan of Malacca, there is no reason to doubt a statement in the "Malay Annals" that it was drawn up for Muzaffar Shah, Sultan of Malacca from 1446 to 1456, the son of Sultan Muhammad by a Tamil, who elevated to the throne by the intrigues of Muslim traders of his mother's race had good reason to introduce a digest grafting the Islamic law of the new Sultanate on to the earlier law of a Hindu court.

Better known as Malacca Laws (*Undang-Undang Melaka*) than by its Arabic title of *Risalat Hukum Kanun*, "A tract on Customary Law", it starts with a preamble of Hindu pattern on the modes of dress and styles of clothing forbidden to all except the ruler, prescribing death for those who dared to wear royal yellow or lift hands in homage to anyone but the

Raja, the confiscation of gold-mounted daggers from those unauthorized to wear them, and the tearing of diaphanous garments off the backs of those not privileged by royal favour to affect such soft luxury. After that, the compiler makes the sweeping statement that death is the punishment for ten offences, a number common in Hindu law: namely, murder, stabbing and hacking; striking; robbery, theft; bringing false charges (*bertudoh-tudohan*); perjury before a judge (*berdusta 'kan hakim*); betraying royal commands (*berjual titah*) and opposing them. Under Hindu law, also, death might be the penalty for those ten offences, though theft of smaller sums might cost the thief only a hand or a foot and the betrayer of royal commands might be let off with the loss of his tongue and with banishment. So, too, for some of the ten offences the Malacca digest goes on to prescribe alternative lesser penalties. The "Malay Annals" tell how Sultan Mahmud had his Laksamana or Admiral castrated for making false charges that led to the execution of Bendahara Mutahir. And according to the digest the betrayer of royal commands might be merely scalped or have his tongue cut off. The compiler also reveals a knowledge of the Hindu and Muslim *lex talionis*, namely the exaction of an eye for an eye and a tooth for a tooth, under which a thief loses not his life but a hand, and he adds correctly that Muslim law does not regard the purloining of garden produce as a crime grave enough to justify such amputation. He explains further that the theft of cattle or poultry from their pens is punishable by fine and restitution under the custom and by restitution only according to Muhammadan law. Both the Malacca and Pahang digests exhibit traces of the Hindu caste system, under which the greater the person offended the greater the offence. And generally both digests are marked by contemporary inconsistencies that left scope for an autocratic ruler to follow customary, Hindu or Muslim law as he pleased. In mediaeval Malacca, therefore, no one can ever have been certain of the provisions of the patriarchal police law, designed, with its public cages of starved and mutilated criminals, to cow a cosmopolitan port mob. The generalization as to the death sentences for ten offences can hardly have exaggerated the disregard for life. The victim of a blow could kill the man who had struck him, any time within three days without being guilty of crime, and if he killed him after that interval he was still only liable to be fined, although Muslim law, as the digest notes, would hold him guilty of murder. Even a slave in Malacca was permitted to avenge assault by a free man by killing his assailant without incurring a charge of culpable homicide. But if one were guilty of a crime punishable by death, Hindu law with its practice of compounding murder by the payment of blood-money made no absolute break with the clement Malay custom of imposing a fine instead of the death sentence, a custom apparently in full force in 18th-century Perak in spite of its patriarchal and aristocratic constitution.

Towards accomplices Malacca exhibited the lenient customary and Muslim attitude. If only one of a gang of burglars entered a house, he alone suffered amputation of a hand; any accomplice had his face smeared with chalk, soot and saffron, and with the stolen goods hung about his neck was gonged round the town, a dish-cover for his umbrella as he sat on a pink buffalo, decked with hibiscus flowers.

To what we term criminal law the Pahang digest of 1596 devotes only a few short sections. The digest was prepared for 'Abd al-Ghaffar, a descendant of Malacca's royal house, ruler of Pahang from 1592 till 1614, a poor creature apparently, despised by his consort's Patani relatives, who, however, as a concession presumably to his pious scruples, killed all the dogs when he visited them. The digest praises this Sultan in Arabic terms, that lead one to expect strict adherence to Muslim law. But what do we find in this digest, which was also a work of legal reference in Perak and Johor? Anyone except a lunatic may be killed for knocking at a door by night. One escorting his women-folk may kill anyone who insults them. A man may kill anyone who improperly abuses his wife. An extraordinarily immoral penalty is laid down for a slave who assaulted a free man, namely that after retaliation in kind he should have his hands nailed down while the free man was at liberty to enjoy his wife, but only until retaliation should be effected! The Malacca digest prescribed amputation of the slave's hand.

In Malacca, if a great chief were condemned for treason, he was allowed to stab himself or get a relative to do it. This, at any rate, was the method by which its last Sultan, Mahmud, rid himself of his relative Bendahara Mutahir. "A commoner," according to Pires' Suma Oriental, "they take into the street and order him to be killed or impaled or burnt alive or beaten on the chest to death, according to the nature of the crime. And the estate of all these people goes to the king if they have no heir in the direct line, and if they have one, he takes the half." These penalties were almost humane compared with the three-hundred and sixty tortures prescribed for traitors in the last section of 'Abd al-Ghaffar's digest, tortures to be followed by quartering. This section gave sanction for the horrible punishments that survived in Pahang until the British period. In 1674 the yearly journal kept by the Dutch Governor at Malacca records how the Sultan of Johor, then in Pahang, had had the hands and feet cut off a Jambi pirate, his back-bone split open, and the wounds smeared with salt and pepper. A Pahang method of execution was to weight the condemned man's body with a stone and drown him. A variation was to fix the nape of the criminal's neck in a cleft branch and tow him in the wake of a boat till he was dead.

Of the date of the supplement to the Pahang digest there is no indication. As a rule, it gives the Muslim penalties for crime. Keeping close to Sunni law-books, it exempts the thief of a small sum from amputation. Under the law of Shafi'i, homicide accompanied by robbery was punishable by death, and the corpse was to be exposed on a cross for three days; the Pahang supplement substitutes for crucifixion the ancient punishment of impaling, borrowed by the Malays from the Hindu as a punishment for robbery, and lays it down that the malefactor be impaled for three days. Another section in direct conflict with the Hindu punishments for treason reproduces the mild Shafi'ite law for the suppression of armed rebellion.

Leniency is the mark of the Ninety-Nine laws of Perak, a digest compiled in the 18th century by Sayids who held the high office of Mantri or Justiciar in that State. The Muslim guilty of homicide was to pay a fine and to provide a buffalo or a white goat or a white camel for the funeral feast. Even an infidel was not to be put to death for homicide. For a first offence a thief might compound, for a second he should lose a finger and for a third be expelled from the parish. As for wounding, if the hurt were above the navel, blood money of $25 was to be paid; if below the navel, $5, and if there were only slight bleeding, an offering of white cloth sufficed. Whatever crime a man committed, these Sayid Justiciars held that, provided he could pay the proper fine, his sins should be pardoned in this world. "Otherwise, of what use would be gold?" It is easy to see how these Sayids bowed to the older tribal views on punishment and how they acquired place and honour.

Yet even these Ninety-Nine Laws of theirs advise that, if evidence is as "dark as a black fowl flying by night", there can, it is true, be no conviction, but the suspected person may be fined or else privily killed! At an autocratic court even a dream might be accounted good evidence. Vaughan, a shipwrecked sailor, held captive in Johor in 1702, saw a Malay creesed and his wife drowned with a stone tied to her neck, because whenever the sick Bendahara went to sleep he dreamt that the couple were trying to strangle him. When evidence was as clear as a "white fowl flying by day", there was still the danger that an aristocratic judge, misled by the casuistry Muslim pundits displayed to impress Malay royalty, might come to a decision so ingenious as to be at once absurd and iniquitous. At a court which we had persuaded the Sultan of Pahang to institute just before the British took over the administration of his State, the heirs of the original owner of a buffalo, sold along with five calves thirty years before, preferred a claim against the purchaser for twenty-two calves born subsequently. All the buffaloes were confiscated by the court as well as the purchaser's other movable property with his house and land, on the ground that he had wounded and seduced a woman twenty years before, a woman who all those years had been his wife!

The supplement to the Pahang digest summarizes the qualifications and number of witnesses demanded by Muhammadan law. But of what use were these rules among people accustomed to prefer circumstantial evidence and in places where a crowd of sycophants would say anything to please their chiefs and a show of independence might lead to a witness being cut down in court for *lèse-majesté?* A man was often not an individual entitled to a fair trial but a *corpus vile* between rival rajas and chiefs. When a pandar for Sultan Mahmud had stabbed an inconvenient husband, the most that ruler of Malacca could do was to contrive his escape, and then years later, when the fellow returned from exile, to send him bound to Sriwa Raja, head of the injured family, with a plea for pardon. Sriwa Raja killed the man with his elephant-goad.

In spite of the injunctions of Islam the Malays, like other Muslims, retained tortures and modes of execution dating from their days of ignorance, more especially their Hindu period. The Malacca digest provides an example of the transition from earlier practices in the contemporary ordeals employed to test veracity. While Muslim missionaries taught that it sufficed to swear with a hand on the pulpit of a mosque, custom still required the litigants to compete at diving or at plunging a hand into boiling water or molten tin, but the potsherd the successful competitor would extract bore an inscription calling on Allah and the four Archangels to reveal which of the litigants spoke the truth. The author of the *Bustan al-Salatin* praised Sultan Iskandar II who ruled Acheh between 1635 and 1641 for abolishing the two old ordeals of immersion in boiling oil and licking red-hot steel.

LEGAL SYSTEMS 105

Torture and execution were the penalties for acts that modern Europe would not consider criminal. The penalty for apostasy from Islam was death. Those taken in adultery might be stoned to death under Muhammadan law. But over the relation of the sexes the adoption of that law was as gradual as in other fields of jurisprudence. Brutal as many of the penalties in the Malacca digest are, its mediaeval customary law was more lenient towards sexual offences than contemporary Muslim practice. Muhammadan law prescribed death by stoning not only for adultery with a married woman but for the married man guilty of fornication (with anyone but a slave), and eighty stripes for any person who falsely charged another with these sexual irregularities, but Malacca custom only fined the libertine and the slanderer.

The Malacca digest contains reminiscences of Hindu marriage by forcible abduction, laying it down that if aware of her betrothal the abductor of an affianced girl was liable to be fined, and if the girl's parents had concealed the betrothal from him, it was they who were to be fined, double the dowry being returned in either case. According to the 18th century Ninety-Nine Laws of Perak, the seducer of a betrothed girl was merely fined and married off, that is, if he could pay the fine and provide double the dowry (half of it for the jilted suitor), though if the seducer could not pay, he was not to be married but banished, beaten and plundered; and if fines were not paid, the woman was to have her head shaved and be pilloried at the door of the mosque.

In the Malacca digest it is stated that by customary law, if a man killed anyone making overtures to his wife or daughter, he was merely fined, and if a man raped a slave-girl, he had only to marry her or be fined, whereas Shafi'ite law would admittedly sentence him to death by lapidation. According to the Pahang digest a married woman was executed for adultery only if her husband and lover killed one another. According to the Ninety-Nine Laws of Perak, if a husband killed his wife's seducer not outright but after delay, he was merely fined. The same Laws allowed a couple

H

guilty of illicit intercourse to marry or settle the matter between themselves.

This condonation of sexual sins, these fines for those able to pay for fornication and for deliberate homicide are quite alien to Muslim law. And again there is the difference between Malay preference for circumstantial evidence and the Muslim's demand for witnesses: the Ninety-Nine Laws required a girl only to produce some piece of a man's trousers for his conviction, and the penalty was marriage. But it is a curious example of the mediaevalisms resuscitated by the Malay Muhammadan Laws Enactment that it makes the marriage of milk-kindred a criminal offence, while according to the Ninety-Nine Laws it sufficed if the respective mothers met and forgave the pair. That is only one item of the mediaeval provisions in a retrograde piece of legislation, which crystallizes an outmoded fanaticism not natural in the Malay.

Different though they were, there are points in common between Malay and Muslim criminal law. Both punished offences against private morality, the Malay law adultery and the highly constructive crime of tribal incest, the Muslim, adultery—and fornication, which in primitive Malay communities was the accepted road to marriage. For both systems murder was an injury to the family of the victim rather than an offence against the state, and both of them allowed monetary compensation in lieu of the death penalty. Although the amputation of a hand was retained from pagan days as the Muslim punishment for theft, the Prophet declared the mutilation even of a mad dog to be unlawful, thereby aligning himself with the primitive Malay who always sought to compound an offence. The penalty for treason against that incarnation of godhead, the Malay Raja, was death, and so was the Muslim penalty for apostasy; but Malays guilty of treason were, like Hindu traitors, impaled, a form of execution unknown to Arabs and showing its place of origin by a Sanskrit name (*sula*). Modern Muslim countries like Turkey and Egypt have abolished the death penalty for apostasy and would not think of stoning to death those taken in adultery or of amputating the hand or foot of a thief, nor do they countenance the compounding of murder. And their example made it easy for the British to drop the deference the East India Company paid to the criminal system of the Kuran and to deal with all crimes by Malays in accordance with the Indian Penal Code. This reform was facilitated by the vagueness of Malay legal knowledge outside Negri Sembilan. Above all, the change was easy because the Malays instinctively preferred a legal system fixed and humane as their primitive custom had been. For it must not be thought, that because so far the authority of old digests has been quoted, therefore the change was in theory only. Begbie, writing in 1828, disproves any such assumption. "The administration of justice at Trengganu," he quotes from an eye-witness, "is distinguished by the same laxity that prevails in all the Malay States. . . . Fining, mutilation and capital punishments are a terror to evil doers, and even of these the former appears to be either unknown or rarely practised. . . . In the case of the first offence, nothing but the restoration of the article itself is required" of a thief, "and a slight reprimand is adjudged: on a repetition of the crime, the thief is sentenced to the loss of a hand and" (? = or)"foot, and although the method of amputation is exceedingly unskilful, the member being severed by a violent blow, the temperate habits of the people generally ensure recovery. The relatives, however, in most cases take off the individual by poison rather than suffer him to remain a living monument of their disgrace. . . . When the offence is of no ordinary dye, death is inflicted, the culprit kneeling on the ground, and the executioner thrusting a *keris* down the suture of the left shoulder-blade, until the point penetrates the heart." In 1958 there still lived an old man who had seen a youth, guilty of *lèse-majesté* by some trivial court intrigue, with his scalp pulled down over his eyes and his body tied to a stake in the Pahang estuary to be drowned by the rising tide. Erring women were the victims of obscene tortures.

It was English jurisprudence that first showed the Malay any distinction between constitutional criminal and civil law. Malay constitutional law was generally commensurate with the ruler's prerogatives in the wearing of clothes and weapons. And both in constitutional and in criminal law Hindu influence is apparently more pronounced than in civil law. For not only was suppression of crime the main object of law in a port kingdom but fines were a profitable source of income to rulers and chiefs. "When some man injures another or a woman," Tomé Pires records, "half the fine goes to the king and half to the complainant. They cannot demand justice without the complainant takes something to the judge, according to the nature of what is demanded. From this the Bendaharas are very rich."

Torts also brought fines and fees, and Malay digests contain many sections dealing with damage to the two commonest forms of property, slaves and crops. The Malacca digest sets forth the customary law dealing with compensation for the killing of slaves and for the death of a slave borrowed, with rewards for the capture of fugitive slaves and the penalty for concealing them. Generally the customary penalties are very different from those of Islamic law. For example. In old Malacca, if a slave were caught thieving and killed without resisting, payment of half his value was the penalty; if a slave were impertinent and were struck and killed, payment of his full value was the penalty. If a free man slapped a slave or abused his wife and was killed, so far from the slave's life being forfeit he was held to have committed no offence. Where Muslim law would demand a life for a life, Malay law considers the interest of the slave-owner. Nor would Muslim law countenance the execution of a man for striking a royal slave for no fault, or the cutting off of a slave's hand for slapping a free man, or the exaction of a fine of half the value of a slave assaulted by another slave, or the exaction from the widow and children of a debt-bondsman of one third of the money he owed his creditor. Nor would it countenance the execution of anyone who stole a royal slave or a nobleman's slave and could not pay a fine of seven times the slave's value if he or she were the property of a ruler or prince, of five times his or her value if the owner were a *biduanda* or *sida-sida*, or of twice his or her value if the owner were a commoner. Yet all these Hindu penalties are prescribed in the Malacca digest and generally repeated or amplified in the Pahang digest. According to the latter any one could escape execution for murder by seeking sanctuary as a royal slave, and if a slave wounded a free man, he too could save his life by seeking that sanctuary, his owner being at liberty to buy him back. Malay slave law must have shocked Muslim missionaries like the Sayid who compiled Perak's Ninety-Nine Laws and hardly mentions slaves. "If a debtor find it hard to pay," says the Kuran, "let his creditor wait till it is easy, but to remit debt in alms were better." Contrast that with the Pahang digest:—"Debts are payable on an agreed date or upon demand. If the agreed date is exceeded by a single day, the debtor may be sent to work on his creditor's mine and if he abscond becomes his creditor's slave. If the debt is payable on demand and the debtor absconds, he becomes a slave, and should he leave his work he may be beaten but not so as to draw blood." According to the same digest, a man harbouring a fugitive slave lost his ears and a woman was shaved and whipped. Malay law further protected the purchaser of any slave suffering from madness, short-sight, asthma or an aneurism, of a pregnant slave, and of a slave notorious for absconding or thieving or betraying a master; laying it down that such a slave could be returned to the vendor within a fixed time. Malay slave law is summed up in the Pahang digest. "The loan of a slave is like the borrowing of a stick or anything else; should anything happen to him, there must be compensation." Malay law looked on the slave not as a human being but as a chattel. Yet over fornication or defamation by slaves or their drunkenness, the supplement to the Pahang digest exactly follows Shafi'ite law, making the penalty half that for a free person.

Another form of property, land, was hardly as valuable as slaves in mediaeval Malaya. And the law relating to land was so familiar to Malays that it occupies little space in the digests. The general principles of customary land tenure are simple. Among the Malays, as among the Hindus and in Burma, Siam and Indo-China, a proprietary right to land was created either by felling forest or by planting land abandoned with no sign of occupation. If the crop were hill rice, bananas, maize, sugarcane and so on, proprietary right lasted for the period of occupation, generally a season or at most two. If fields were irrigated for rice, the right lasted for the period of occupation and three years afterwards. If the land were planted as an orchard, the right lasted as long as any fruit-trees remained. Were a man to plant fruit-trees on land belonging to another or to irrigate it for rice-planting, and were the owner to complain, then one third of the crop was adjudged to the owner and two thirds to the occupier; though if occupation had been granted by a chief or ruler, a prior owner had no claim unless the ruler admitted it on his appeal. A man might borrow, rent or buy land not cultivated by its owner, and it was sometimes held that no owner could object to the occupation of uncultivated land unless it adjoined other land of his or were kept fallow for a purpose. But rent paid to an owner for land leased had to be in money and not, say, in a quarter of the crop. The term owner of land is not strictly accurate, as no Malay could claim to hold any property in land approaching our freehold or fee simple tenure, though ground planted or built on became a species of property and the interest in it was transferable. The price or rent paid was, however, not for the soil but for produce and buildings. The Perak term for the transfer of land was the return of the vendor's outlay (*pulang belanja*). And Kedah laws laid it down that when a holding was sold, the trees were to be valued at 25 cents each and the total of their value was the price of the land. Again, if a proprietor raised money by hypothecating (*jual janji*) his rights on condition that he could resume them by paying his debt, it was not property in the soil that passed but usufruct in lieu of the interest forbidden by Muhammadan law. If the borrower wanted to retain usufruct, he became the tenant of his creditor, and the rent paid by him in cash or kind took the place of interest. If a man hypothecated an orchard planted with fruit-trees (but not one planted with coconut or betel palms) and they did not bear for years, then the creditor could claim double the money lent. The agriculturist was conservative and had fewer Muslim missionaries than courts and ports had to teach him all the ramifications of Islamic law on usury, nor could he discriminate between usufruct and ownership. The Minangkabau tribal sayings naïvely viewed virgin forest and wide plains as the property of the birds.

When Hindu Rajas took the place of Malay aboriginal chiefs, they were not so simple. As in India they claimed not only a right to one tenth of the crop and the right to collect taxes and exact forced labour, but also the right to dispose of abandoned land and land to which there was no heir. Thus arose the doctrine, recognized by the British, that the soil belonged to the ruler, the peasant never having claimed more than usufruct dependent on occupation. So if a Raja granted an area to a chief, he really transferred his right to the tithes and taxes on that area and to the disposal of abandoned or forfeited lands.

The one right a Raja found it very difficult to enforce was the collection of the tithe. In 1884 the only area where Sir William Maxwell had seen a tenth of the grain collected was Krian, a district regarded as the personal property of the Sultan of Perak and a district from which the export of most of the grain made collection possible. The Pahang digest declares it no crime to kill a man resisting the collection of tithes, which with the coming of Islam often became identified with the Muslim religious tithe or *zakat:* in 1880 the Perak government decided that, as Kathis were paid officials, they were no longer to accept *zakat*.

Outside Negri Sembilan there was no common ownership or usufruct of land by groups or tribes. But custom decreed that the individual should have regard to a neighbour's rights. If a spring yielded more water than the Pahang farmer needed for his own family and cattle, he had to share it with others. All the digests follow the precedent set by Hindu and Muslim jurists of handling such torts as trespasses on land and an owner's responsibility for damage done by his cattle to man or crop. If in old Malacca a man set fire to a clearing newly felled by someone else or by himself and partners and it was not a clean burn, he had to chop and pile the branches on half the area or, if the occupier were a chief, on the whole area. The Malacca digest lays it down that anyone who plucks fruits in a neglected orchard is liable to pay the owner one third of their value. It prescribes that if a buffalo tethered on a public road kills anyone, the owner has to pay the money equivalent for a life, and that if the animal merely wounds, a fine meets the case. If the buffalo is tethered in the jungle, the owner has only to slaughter the beast, whether its victim is killed or wounded. According to the Pahang digest, if one of the joint occupiers of land failed to fence his portion and damage ensued, he was responsible for it all, but according to the Ninety-Nine Laws the Perak farmer defrayed one third of the damage and the owner of the beast two thirds. If a buffalo were killed by a Pahang farmer or his men for damaging unfenced crops at night, he had to pay the beast's value in full; if a buffalo was killed for damaging fenced crops at night, in Kedah it was no offence but in Pahang opinions differed as to whether half the value of the buffalo had to be paid or its full value minus the value of the damaged crop. If a Pahang peasant killed a beast for damaging crops by day, twice its value had to be paid to the owner, or if it were notoriously vicious, half only with a set-off of the value of the damaged crop. According to the Ninety-Nine Laws if a Perak holding were strongly fenced, a trespassing buffalo might be killed or kept unless compensation for damage were paid. Kedah laws of 1667 favour the rice-planter against the owner of a buffalo. The law of torts was not uniform in the different Malay states.

Another form of property is credits, and on this form the

Pahang digest of 1596 has one section. "Debts are of two kinds. In one kind, if the creditor is at fault by assault or forcible molestation (of a woman), the debt is reduced by the amount of the penalty (for his offence). Similarly a debt may be reduced by the amount of a dowry. Debts for overseas transactions may never exceed the original sum. There are also two kinds of pledges. The sum due on those that bear interest may never exceed 100 per cent. (*ganda*). As for pledges that carry no interest, when the debt has reached the value of the pledge, the debtor must redeem it or have so much of the pledge sold as will settle the debt; if the pledge is worth less than the money lent, the deficit becomes a debt." This section with its recognition of the interest forbidden by Muhammad ends with the incongruous adjuration that Muslims must be merciful to borrowers and debtors. The rule that interest may not exceed 100 per cent. is Hindu. And there is another case in which Malay custom follows Hindu law. A man will charge his land to a creditor allowing him to enjoy the profits or part of the profits of the crop, such profits not to be placed against the money owed but to be in lieu of interest, until the debt is repaid in full. Here is a clear case of evading the Muslim ban against taking interest.

The Malacca digest has a section on the relation of principal and agent. The supplement to the Pahang digest goes much further in legal technicalities, following the practice of Muslim lawyers in including such subjects as sales of land with its immovables and with its permanent or temporary crops, the return of goods purchased with a flaw, pledges, wages and payment for job-work, renting houses, gifts, admissions, the finding of goods on a road or in the forest, apostasy, intentional omission of obligatory prayers and the rules of Holy War in "a transitory world which the Creator esteems so little that He leaves its riches in the hands of the infidel". To enhance the Muslim colouring of his work the author of the Pahang supplement writes of the number and age of camels to be surrendered for blood-money.

In mediaeval Malacca and Pahang, as proprietorship of land carried no possession of the soil, there was strictly no immovable property, and, to judge from the Ninety-Nine Laws of Perak, the distribution of movable property and of proprietary right in land on death or divorce remained a matter of local traditional custom outside the cognizance of the digests. "When some person or merchant dies without an heir in the direct line, the king takes his estate; and if the dead man has made an heir, then they divide the estate between them. First, however, they pay out the alms and the funeral expenses from the total amount, and any debts the dead man owed are paid off." It is Tomé Pires who tells us this practice of mediaeval Malacca, and not the digest. Perhaps it was the spread of Islam even to remote districts that made the compiler of the Ninety-Nine Laws an innovator, who introduced sections on marriage and divorce, dowries and the division of property, the result still being a mixture of Muslim and customary law. He tells us how in deference to Malay custom a woman on divorce takes the homestead, and when the estate of a deceased person is divided, house and garden and household furniture are allotted to the female heirs and rice-fields and mines and weapons to the male. But as late as 1878 the Perak State Council had to admit that most Perak law was still "unwritten, though generally understood and appearing to differ little from the code of laws formerly in force in Malay kingdoms." In theory Muslim law covers inheritance and distribution of property on divorce, but in spite of Islam the equitable and practical principles of Malay traditional custom were too ingrained in the Malay mind to be abandoned. The peasant refused, for example, to accept the Muhammadan law that one eighth of her deceased husband's property was enough for the support of a widow (with child), and gave her from one half to a third. And it was idle for the Perak State Council in 1907 to try to compromise with the *hukum shara'* by applying its general principle of inheritance, that a man's share is twice that of a woman, to the division in divorce cases of the property acquired by a couple during marriage. The peasants often refused to admit that two thirds should go to the man and one third to the wife, and Kathis and headmen supported them in the witness-box. Then in 1927 the Supreme Court ruled that oral evidence on the law of the land was inadmissible. How, then, were officials and judges to discover law not written down and only "very generally understood"? An enactment had to be passed enabling a statement to be submitted to the Ruler in Council for a decision on any moot point. This is likely to fortify Muslim law against the custom. It is possible that increase in the value of land may lead eventually to acceptance of the Muslim principle that a man should get double the woman's share, when land is got and cultivated by their joint efforts, one third of the property being ample for her support. But from villages on the Perak river there is abundant evidence that on divorce half the landed property acquired during wedlock goes even to an unfaithful wife, if she helped to cultivate it, and one third only if she did not help, and that on a husband's death the land is similarly divided, the balance devolving on all the deceased's children irrespective of whether they are the children of his surviving widow or of a previous marriage. A similar practice obtains in Selangor, Pahang and Trengganu and probably in all the States.

"Apart from these rights of widows and divorceés" an expert authority, Mr. Justice A. N. Taylor, has written (1948), "I think not very much of the ancient law of property survives in the northern states. . . . The law of inheritance is now the Muhammadan law. . . . The result is fantastic. An estate consists not of the property of the family but of the interests registered in the name of the deceased, perhaps two lots of three acres each and a half share in a third lot. . . . The District Officer usually asks the Kathi an abstract question such as—'What is the division between a widow, a son, two daughters and the father?' " And the Kathi works out that "each daughter inherits 17/96 of each of the first two lots and an undivided 17/192 share of the third, and as the younger daughter is probably an infant, her shares must be protected by caveats. . . . Some of the co-owners will live at a distance from the land. Are the remainder to cultivate it and keep accounts of the costs and profits? ... The cumulative effect of these caveats and unmanageable fractions is to impose a restriction on sale of the land far more onerous than what custom," in Negri Sembilan, "imposes on ancestral land." The problem is grave. Nor should it have arisen, seeing that in cases of guardianship the Supreme Court has not hesitated to support Malay custom against Muhammadan law by appointing women to be guardians. The trouble arose from calling Kathis as experts on a personal law, which before their intervention was based mainly on custom. Even now it is a mixture of custom and Muhammadan law.

The Kedah laws of A.D. 1650 are little more than port regulations. They are the oldest Malay port laws extant and the fullest. The fixing of harbour dues and market prices had been part of the functions of an Indian king from the time of Chandra Gupta. And these Kedah regulations closely resemble those of the Great Moguls recorded in the Tarikh-i-Tahiri, including as they do provisions for a poll-tax on immigrants, port dues on ships from Gujerat and Kalinga, the collection by the harbour-master of money due to trading captains, the duty payable for the import and export of slaves and for the export of tin and elephants, ships' manifests, standard weights and measures, and the reception of envoys and their missives. The Kedah jurist complacently remarks that established laws encourage foreign trade, but these Kedah regulations make it clear that the trader was fleeced from the moment of his arrival until he sailed away. Presents of the cloth that formed the Indian cargoes had to be made to the Sultan, the harbour-master, the warden of the port, the police and innumerable satellites. Ships from Perak gave presents of tin slabs. In addition there were fees for counting each bale of cloth, fees for storing bales even when they were not stored, import duty to be paid on every bale, presents at opening each bale, fees for pilotage, port dues on entry and exit, fees for witnessing the sale of goods. And in 1650 there was little amusement in the port to counteract the visitor's gloom at this reception. For the regulations go on to say that gaming, cock-fighting, opium-smoking and drinking were all forbidden. Anyone feeding in public during Ramadhan was beaten or else forced to eat grass in front of the court. And at the discretion of the Raja any commoner abducting the daughter or debt-slave of another was liable to be impaled, while a nobleman got off with the Malay equivalent for being tarred and feathered and with being led thus humiliated round the port for seven days, mounted on a buffalo with his face to the tail.

In his initial treaty with Great Britain each of the Rulers reserved for the Malays the interpretation of their own religion and custom. At the very outset, however, the outmoded cruelty of Muslim criminal law, the variety of customary penalties for crimes and torts, and the impossibility of reconciling the Muslim demand for witnesses with the Malay acceptance of circumstantial evidence were practical difficulties that made the Sultans glad to follow in the footsteps of Turkey and Egypt and to adopt the Indian Penal Code and a Law of Evidence that was a compromise between their two discrepant systems. These changes were easier because, while the Kuran laid down rules for marriage, divorce and inheritance, Islamic law has covered only part of the field of penal jurisdiction, and anticipated neither political developments nor the growth of big business.

But the Muslim world has not yet agreed to admit any distinction between crime and sin, between theft from a shop and failure to pay alms or attend the mosque on Friday. Accordingly in 1948, the Chief Kathi of Kelantan fined 14 men and 2 women $15 each, with imprisonment in default of payment, for their refusal to pay *fitrah*, that is, to make the charitable offering of rice to feast the poor at the end of the fasting month. The modernist may want to distinguish between duty to God and obligations to society, but for any such change Muslim opinion must be unanimous, and so far in Malaya as elsewhere that opinion has agreed to the exercise of human judgment only when a return to primitive practice is advocated. It is most regrettable that this permitted the zeal of a Sultan now dead to restore in the peninsula mediaeval legislation fining Muslims who may eat or drink in public during Ramadhan and penalizing the few Malay women who may cohabit with infidels and pagans. Not only are these restrictions contrary to modern ideas of liberty, but they put a Gestapo weapon into the hands of the police. Such legislation strikes the British as so preposterous that I heard a member of Parliament cite it as an adequate excuse for requiring the Rulers' signature to the MacMichael agreement.

III Maritime Law

From mediaeval Malacca comes a digest of Maritime Law (*Undang-Undang Laut*) put together for the use of Bugis trading ships. The "Malay Annals" ascribe its compilation to Sultan Muzaffar Shah (1446–1456 A.D.) though they (p. 99) interpolate the name of Sultan Mahmud. It begins with definitions of the duty of officers and crew. The captain is King. The steersman is Bendahara, that is, Prime Minister. The seaman responsible for sounding and for the anchor is the ship's Temenggong, or Police Chief, who is also maintainer of discipline. The discipline of a Malay crew banded together to face the dangers of the sea must have antedated the Hindu period and was very different from the harsh rule of a cosmopolitan port. If a sailor disobeyed the boatswain, the ship's Temenggong administered seven strokes, but he was not allowed to lift his arm. A sailor who set light to ship's tackle by failing to quench his galley-fire received two strokes. A sailor who singed the anchor rope got as many strokes as there were severed strands. If cargo had to be thrown over in a storm, the owner of the junk had to make good the loss of capital, unless he had consulted and received the assent of all on board who were partners in the venture. Other sections prescribe regulations for a ship's safety, including the provision of an opium-pipe to keep the watch awake, the shares of trade allowed to officers and crew, fares, the charges for salvage and rescues, and the penalties for mutiny, sexual offences, assaults and thefts on board. Like the *Risalat Hukum Kanun*, this maritime digest long survived, and it attracted the attention of Sir Stamford Raffles, founder of Singapore, who translated one recension. There is a Johor version apparently compiled about 1789, enlarged and refined with principles pushed to ultimate conclusions in the way Malay casuists love. The last section of this Johor version reads: "If a man fishes with hook and line from the bows of a vessel at anchor and the line is carried down towards the stern and grasped by anyone and the fisherman mistake the resistance for the tug of a fish and pull it and the person be hooked, his catch shall become his property, even if it be the captain's concubine." [1]

[1] Since this chapter was written, I have found in Raffles MS. 33 in the Library of the Royal Asiatic Society, London, a digest compiled apparently under the Bugis influence of 18th century Selangor. It prescribes, that at divorce by mutual consent, property jointly acquired be divided equally. If a wife was divorced for no fault, she got two-thirds of such property or " according to some authorities " all ; and should there be a deferred dowry unpaid, the man could give up child or children instead.

If a wife wanted divorce from a husband guiltless of offence under religious and customary law, she had to return her dowry or buy his consent for *sa-tahil sa-paha*, departing with only her clothes. If the man's conduct was intolerable though not contrary to Islamic law, she had to return only half her dowry and renounce any claim to property jointly acquired. An adulteress, if a free woman, was to be strangled; though if she survived being strangled thrice, she became the property of the ruler.

7 ECONOMIC SYSTEMS

WHEN British protection began, the Malay in many States had hardly yet discarded his nomadic instincts, still clinging to coast and estuary, still a fisherman and a pirate, an agriculturist of necessity rather than liking, who felled the forest to plant hill rice, took a crop or two and passed on.

Civil war, tyranny and bad administration had taken the heart out of the peasant. Begbie has told how on the islands off Singapore all stimulus to industry was destroyed by the rapacity of the chiefs, who compelled their subjects "to part with *agar-agar*" or sea-weed for jellies, "and *bêche de mer*, the principal products, for an inconceivably small sum." Newbold has noted how in the '30s of the 19th century the population of Muar was reduced to 2,400 "through the mis-government and apathy of the feudal sovereign; owing to which perpetual broils exist among the petty chiefs, causing insecurity of person and of property, and eventually driving out of the country all the cultivating and trading classes of the community. The honest peasant, in many instances, is compelled from sheer necessity to turn robber; and the coasts, instead of being crowded with fishermen, swarm with pirates. These remarks, indeed, may be extended to the whole of the Peninsula." Writing at the same period Munshi 'Abdullah has left a worm's eye view of similar conditions in Trengganu. "Four or five fellows came and invited me to talk, asking news of Singapore. I told them of the freedom and comfort under British rule, and they begged me to take them for my servants, since they could no longer endure the tyranny of Malay rule. 'Every day,' they said, 'we have to work for the Raja at our own cost and without food being supplied to ourselves or our families. Our boats, crops and live-stock are liable to be seized by the Raja without payment. If the Raja wants our property or our daughters, we cannot withstand him. If we object, we are stabbed to death. Try to emigrate and we are killed, if caught, and our property is confiscated.' " Even the Malay system of taxation encouraged reckless improvidence and discouraged thrift and enterprise. Cock-fighting won the chiefs popularity and filled their coffers. In Kedah there was a tax on every plough, in Pahang on coconut oil.

Yet, in spite of all, the Malays like other races had an economic system. And it depended on (a) the catching of fish and planting of food-stuffs for home consumption, (b) the collection of tin and jungle-produce and later of things like dried fish and copra for export, and (c) the marketing and trade of middlemen who in large transactions used always to be rulers and chiefs and in small, peasants male and female.

As early as the 8th century Kuala Selinsing in Perak traded in beads. By the 15th century elephants were exported by the Sultans of Malacca as presents for the Hinduized rulers of Majapahit. And in 1771 the Sultan of Kedah sold to Chulias and exported to the Coromandel coast about seventy elephants a year, thereby getting the chief part of his revenue, which to increase by trading he took in the form of blue cloth and white cloth. But except for the capture of these elephants which Hindu mahouts trained for the Sultans of Malacca and which the rulers of Kedah and Perak used to export to India during the 17th and 18th centuries and perhaps later, trapping for the civilised Malays was only a domestic industry with no commercial end. For centuries the object of the Malay trapper has been only to destroy civet-cat and squirrel in his orchard, rats and pigs in his rice-field, deer in his gardens and rubber estates, and the tiger whenever he was a man-eater. Traps of rattan and bamboo that occur among all Indonesians were the oldest inventions of his race. Caltrops of bamboo cut sharp as a spear protect his rice-fields and are fixed at the bottom of pits dug for tigers and pig. Traps of wood of the mouse-trap pattern have a Sanskrit name and traps involving the use of netting were perhaps of Indian origin. The art of capturing and training elephants has a vocabulary partly Sanskrit and partly Mon-Annam and Siamese.

Fishing is the other most primitive Malay industry and is certainly one of the most specialized for a race of people who are not generally specialists. The earliest method of fishing must have been by rattan traps, as used by the aborigines of the peninsula who have no string-nets, and Malays living on rivers still set traps of this type in the rapid current, with barbed thorns to prevent the escape of their catch or with rattan springs to yank the fish out of the water. Angling with a rattan line and bone hook goes back to prehistoric times and in some parts of Perak the word for a rod is still the Sakai *baur*, though modern angling with or without rods postulates the bronze and iron age with its metal hooks. Among the varieties of Malay angling is an ingenious one that occurs in several parts of the world where a kite is flown on the line to keep it bobbing. From fish-spears of sharpened bamboo or whittled bone have been developed metal spears barbed and unbarbed, tridents, and harpoons with detachable barbed heads. All these methods of fishing are domestic and not commercial. But from their primitive riverine traps of rattan the Malays long since developed large sea-traps of stakes and rattan screens that head the fish into enclosures or cut them off in shallow water. Another great advance was associated with the introduction of twine perhaps by the Hindus, enabling the manufacturer of drift-nets, drag-nets, lift-nets, and fixed purse-nets. Even the cast-net has a Sanskrit name. Later some types of net were copied from Portuguese and Chinese models. This variety of fishing appliances and a great variety of fishing boats not only show the importance of the pursuit in the economy of the coastal Malay but are evidence of Malay cleverness and adaptability.

Chinese annals tell how the Celates or proto-Malays of mediaeval Malacca "many of them live from fishing, for which purpose they go out to sea in canoes made of a single tree". And sea-fishing has come to be the most interesting and complex of the industries of the civilised Malay. The fisherman generally has to borrow to buy a boat and tackle or to buy a share in a boat and net, paying what is in fact

Fishermen, Trengganu

[face p. 122

though not in Malay theory interest on his loan. Sea-fishing with large nets involves the co-operation of large crews and a complicated distribution of the day's earnings to owner, crew and the carrier of the fish to shore as well as the distribution of 20 to 50 fish to each of those persons for domestic consumption. The fish not sold locally needs outlay and labour to dry and cure. All of it requires so many middlemen for its distribution that in Kelantan there were in 1937 apart from retailers 325 fish-dealers, whose ranks included retired or unsuccessful fishermen, agriculturists, a medicine-man, coconut planters and so on. It is remarkable that in such circumstances the Malays of Kelantan and Trengganu have managed to keep fishing and nearly all the selling of fish in their own hands. On the west coast the Malay fisherman has too often become a wage-earner in the pay of Chinese fish-curers.

The size of the industry is considerable and with the aid of European science and increasing demand is likely to grow. Before rubber was planted in Kelantan, fish in 1914 amounted to 14 per cent. of the State's export trade, and in 1930, before iron-ore was mined in Trengganu, fish formed 28½ per cent. of its export trade. In 1939 the marine produce exported from Trengganu was valued at £99,661, not including fish consumed by the local population. The net earnings of individual fishermen before the war were estimated at £1 a month on the east coast and £1 6s. 0d. on the west, and these figures would show an income hardly to be compared with the £1 8s. 0d. to £1 15s. 0d. of the estate cooly and certainly not with with £16 or £20 a month that a Malay planter with two sons could get from his latex at 1s. 2d. a lb. on five acres of rubber-land. But even the whole-time fisherman has other sources of income in the coconut and areca palms and vegetables of his holding, while his wife may weave or make mats or be a market-woman. It is calculated that before the Japanese war the east coast fisherman's weekly purchases for a family of three cost only $1.20 (2s. 9d.), which was mainly due to the traditional diet. When the half-caste Munshi 'Abdullah with his Tamil upbringing visited Kelantan and Trengganu he could not understand why not one in ten Malays liked meat, poultry, eggs, butter and milk but preferred shrimp paste, salt-fish, cockles and durian conserved with prawns, the immemorial food of the coastal tribes. With an average capital of £5 invested in fishing, the Malay of Kelantan and Trengganu got by a year's labour about £12. Meagre as the fisherman's takings were, he led a free and independent life, and the fishing industry as a whole made a sufficient margin of profit to maintain and increase its capital and for some of its members to buy land or jewellery.

Equally important in Malay economy is the planting of rice, and the history of its evolution is not without interest.

According to Portuguese accounts, Malacca was chosen as a settlement on the advice of proto-Malay sea-gypsies or Celates, who were pirates and fishermen with huts for their families on land, and who in return for this service received from its first ruler, the Parameswara, great hereditary titles and offices. It is, therefore, hardly surprising if Malacca then produced little or no rice. Chinese annals tell us in 1416 "the fields are not fertile and produce little rice, for which reason the people do not occupy themselves much with agriculture", and again under the date 1537 it is reiterated that Malacca produced no rice. But before 1512 Muar, according to Tomé Pires, had enough rice for its 2000 people and Bruas had plenty of rice. However, for the bulk of its rice mediaeval Malacca depended on imports from Pasai and Java. Chinese annals of the Ming period (1368—1643) record that Johor too produced no rice, and even Perak in the 17th century was exchanging tin for rice, salt, sugar, onions, leeks and pepper. By the time Newbold wrote his book on "The British Settlements in the Straits of Malacca" (1839) Perak was growing more than enough rice for its 35,000 Malays, and Rembau, Naning and Johol produced a surplus for export to Malacca, though Pahang looked to Singapore and Malacca for supplies, Sungai Ujong was bartering tin for rice, opium, salt, tobacco and cloth, and districts of Selangor were exchanging pine-apples, plantains and yams for rice, salt and tobacco. Only Kedah, Newbold points out, "in common with Patani, possessed a greater number of open plains and *sawah* than any of the other Malay States; consequently its facilities for producing wet grain were greater. The produce of rice formerly exceeded the internal consumption by about the annual average of 2,500 *koyan*, which were exported to Pinang and the neighbouring ports."

The people of Kedah and of Kelantan (about which Newbold knew little) must have planted wet rice from the days when they were subject to Sri Vijaya, and later they came under the influence first of the Javanese of Majapahit and then of the Thai, both of them expert at irrigating ricefields. It must have been for want of rice-plains that until the rise of Malacca in the 15th century southern Malaya remained almost uninhabited except for a few ports for the collection of tin and jungle produce. Then the founding of Malacca brought the Minangkabaus, again expert planters, to Negri Sembilan and to Jelai in Pahang. One may surmise on the evidence that it was never the coastal Malay, close relative of the Orang Laut, who opened wet rice-fields in Malaya, at any rate unless and until he came under other influences. Malaya's wet-rice area was augmented in 1906 by the British irrigation of 50,000 acres in Krian, which were planted up by immigrant Malays, and a committee appointed in 1930 gave the perhaps sanguine estimate that Malaya's potential rice-land still amounted to 600,000 or even 1,000,000 acres, that is, to more than the 700,000 acres then under cultivation. The rice famine, that between 1917 and 1922 prevented the import of grain from Burma, brought home to the people of Malaya the need for a large home crop. The government exerted itself. In 1925, after a decade of experiment, out of 1300 strains of rice British agriculturists selected 16 pedigree lines calculated to increase the crop by 30 per cent., and experimental stations and plots were started for tests and demonstrations and the issue of seed to the Malays. Official rat-catchers were appointed for large areas, and traps and insecticides were distributed at agricultural shows and village fairs. By 1937 the total area in British Malaya with special irrigation systems for rice-planting was just over 142,000 acres. The high price of rubber however retarded padi-planting, though by 1937 Malaya produced 36 per cent. of its rice, an improvement due partly to an increase of the rice-area by 32,000 acres since 1930 and even more to the use of selected seed. Europeans especially are apt to blame the Malay for lack of energy in developing rice-areas, overlooking the point that it is not laziness but common-sense to prefer to plant an isolated holding with rubber rather than to prepare it for an uncertain rice-crop exposed to the hazards of pests and drought.

The average Malay holding is about $2\frac{1}{2}$ acres, which will provide food for a family of six and leave some surplus that can be sold to buy clothes. But rice is not the sole crop of such a holding. Chinese annals tell us of Malacca in 1416: "the people have sugar-cane, plantains, jack-fruit, onion, ginger, leek, mustard, gourds and melons. Cattle, goats, fowl and duck are few and very dear, one buffalo costing a *kati* of silver. There are no donkeys or horses." A later Chinese account, dated 1537, says that for fowls, geese and ducks the people of Malacca depended on foreign countries. Conditions have not changed greatly down the centuries. When in 1830 Munshi 'Abdullah visited the east coast of Malaya, he noted how holdings were planted with coconut and areca palms and how from up-river came aroids, sweet potatoes, yams, bananas and sugar-cane; the people kept buffaloes and goats, a few cattle (except in Kelantan where they were plentiful) and a few ducks and chicken. To-day there are still no donkeys and except in the towns no ponies. Buffaloes are slaughtered only for Malay feasts and are reared mostly for ploughing and for hauling timber. The Malay fowl is now ubiquitous, a lean underfed bird of no breed, whose future a veterinary department has in hand. The rearing of ducks and geese is left to the Chinese. So is regular market gardening. For the Malay holding is still an unkempt tangle of vegetables, bananas, jack-fruit, gourds, onion, ginger, sugar-cane and chillies, flourishing where there is not too dense a shade from coconut and areca palms, fruit trees and rubber. Para rubber belongs to the present century and there are vegetables and fruit-trees unknown to the Malay's remote ancestors. The manggo with its clean aromatic taste of dilute turpentine has an Indian name and origin. The sapodilla, the soursop, the bullock's heart, the custard-apple, the guava and the papaya were introduced by the Portuguese from tropical America.

Of miscellaneous crops, after Acheh in the 17th century destroyed the pepper-fields of Kedah, coconuts and rubber now arrogate to themselves the name of major industries. When the British entered the Malay States, there were places where even special inducements failed to encourage the planting of more coconut palms than were required for personal needs, the experience of continued peace being needed to bring home to the Malay that the fruit of his toil no longer lay at the mercy of an invader's axe. But before the Japanese war, there were about 300,000 Asiatic small holders, the majority of them Malays, owning properties worth about £15,000,000; and the Agricultural Department had persuaded many Malays to prepare their own copra instead of selling their crops to Chinese middlemen. Malaya had become the world's fourth largest exporter of copra and coconut oil.

Except for the Malay cultivation of rice and coconuts, agriculture in Malaya was negligible until in 1877 rubber seedlings, sent from Kew to the Botanic Gardens at Singapore, led to the birth of Malaya's rubber industry. When the growth of the motor industry raised the price of rubber to 12s. a lb., Malays not only felled new clearings but cut down their fruit trees and planted up even rice-fields with the new tree. By 1937 Asiatics owned 53.7 per cent. of the planted area, and at least half the proprietors of the 1,275,822 acres of small holdings under rubber were believed to be Malays. Displacement of natural by synthetic rubber would involve loss of livelihood or a lowering of the standard of living for the majority of Malay agriculturists.

Centuries before rubber or even coconuts were cultivated for the market, the arrival of Indian merchants had caused the Malay to add to his precarious means of subsistence by selling tin, gold and jungle produce. Under the date A.D. 1416 the Chinese annals tell how Malacca produced "lignum aloes, *damar*, tin, etc. When they have made a boat, they use *damar* to smear over the seams and then the water cannot get through: much of it is collected for foreign countries. . . . In the forest is a tree called sago which is soaked and pounded; small globes of it are dried in the sun and sold for food. The natives make intoxicating *kajang* (= *nipah*) wine. They make fine mats for sale." Under the date 1436 the Chinese record how Pahang exported lignum aloes, camphor, tin and sappan wood for dyeing and how the people made toddy and boiled salt out of sea-water. Pahang then imported gold, silver, coloured silks, Java cloths, copper and ironware and gongs. Early Johor exported rhinoceros' horns, ivory, tortoise-shell, camphor, dragon's blood, tin, wax, mats, cotton, areca-nut, *agar-agar* or edible sea-weed, edible birds' nests and mangosteens. In Newbold's day (1839) Johor produced gold, tin, ivory, ebony, fragrant eagle-wood, sappan wood, a little camphor and bees'-wax; Batu Pahat exported annually about 400 *pikul* of ebony, 1000 bundles of rattan, 15 *pikul* of aloe wood, some ivory, *damar*, wax and sandal-wood. According to Newbold, Trengganu exported, besides 7000 *pikul* of tin annually, ivory, gold, pepper, camphor and *gambir*, and it had formerly exported 2000 *pikul* of coffee. For Perak rattans are mentioned as one of the principal exports along with tin and rice. Pahang was exporting a yearly average of 1000 *pikul* of tin and 300 lbs. troy of gold and was importing opium, silk, tobacco, salt, cloths, ironware, agricultural implements and tools. The people of Sungai Ujong bartered their tin for rice, opium, salt, tobacco, cloths, oil and shells for making lime. It would be tedious to continue with statistics for all the States. The exports show on what the Malay depended to supplement his bare livelihood, and the imports show how his supplementary earnings were spent on foodstuffs like salt, which inland districts lacked, on cloths and on such luxuries as opium and tobacco.

A gold pin like a drawing pin was found in a stone cist or slab grave at Tegurwangi in south Sumatra along with the beads that with pottery and bronze and iron tools occur in this type of grave in Perak, Sumatra and Java, and it has been surmised that the use of such graves cannot be earlier than the bronze or Dong-so'n age, that is, cannot be dated earlier than five centuries before Christ. If so, the old gold workings at Selinsing, a place not far from the Jelai river in Pahang, may be mines dug by the Yue and the Cham bronze-workers, or, if the cist-graves are modelled on Han forms, by Chinese of the Han period (206 B.C.—A.D. 200). They are certainly not Siamese mines as Malays call them. Tomé Pires tell how in 1512 Pahang had gold dust in good quantity but of less value than that from Minangkabau, and Barbosa (1518) talks of Pahang as having much base gold. Pahang gold was taken overland to Malacca in those days, and Godinho de Eredia gave sensational details of a vein of gold a yard wide being sent to Joas de Silva, Governor of Malacca, in 1586. The miners then were expert Minangkabaus, who from about 1550 had poured into Pahang through Ulu Muar and were mining gold on the Jelai and its tributaries. In 1727 Captain Alexander Hamilton described how Malays in Pahang dived for gold, and he gave the output as eight hundredweight in some years or about half the highest recorded output in 1897. In his book published in 1839 Newbold wrote: "The annual produce of gold from the Malay peninsula, on a rough estimate, amounts to 19,800 ounces. It is chiefly got at Ulu Pahang, Trengganu, Kelantan, Johol, Gemencheh, Jelai, Pekan and Batu Moring and other places at the foot of Mt. Ophir." There is no reason to suppose that gold deposits are exhausted, but rubber and prosperity have made Malays neglect an industry on which the poor nature of the ground allowed very small returns. Small as those returns were, in former days they helped some Malays to eke out their meagre subsistence.

Tin-mining in Malaya also goes back to the bronze age, having been practised (p. 10) by immigrants from Indo-

China a few hundred years before Christ. Those Yues and Chams were followed by Indians who between the 5th and 9th centuries A.D. left Buddhist bronze images in Perak. In the 9th century even Arabs were trading with Kedah for tin. Then soon after the founding of Malacca Chinese annals under 1416 record from there that, "tin is found in two places in the mountains. . . . It is cast into small blocks weighing 1 *kati* 8 *tahil* or 1 *kati* 4 *tahil* official weight. Ten pieces are bound with rattan to form a small bundle, while forty make a large. They use these pieces of tin instead of money." Thirty years later the Chinese mention tin as an export from Pahang, and annals of the Ming period record how it was among the exports from Johor and how the people of Malacca occupied themselves chiefly with washing tin and fishing. Tomé Pires writing in 1512 cites Mjmjam (? Manjong) as the payer to Malacca of the largest tribute in tin, then Selangor and Bruas and lastly in one class Perak, Bernam, Klang and Sungai Ujong. Soon afterwards when Manjong vanished from history and a great flood robbed Bruas of its port facilities, Perak came to be the largest producer of tin down to modern times. For more than a century Portugal tried to enforce a monopoly in the purchase of this Perak and other Malayan tin, which meant an inadequate price for the Malays. After their failure the 17th century saw Perak and Kedah saved from the stranglehold of Dutch monopolists by the rivalry of Achehnese, Indian, Javanese and English traders. But in 1699 the Dutch collected in Perak the "extraordinary quantity" of 770,000 lbs. or more than double the estimate of its annual output given by Godindo de Eredia a century earlier, though far less than Newbold's estimate of 1,133,200 lbs. in 1839. For the founding of Penang in 1786 had introduced free trade into Malaya and stimulated output. Newbold talks of tin being exported from all the Malay States except Kedah which he must have overlooked. Kelantan he gives as producing 400,000 lbs. a year, a total next highest to Perak's output. By Newbold's time there were Chinese miners in all the western states and probably everywhere. At Lukut, for example, there were 300 or more Chinese diggers. In

Sungai Ujong these Chinese miners were then paid $5 to $8 a month but Malays only $3 to $5, being too lazy to dig deep. Besides, while the Chinese handled large bellows to smelt the ore, the Malays were mostly content with a hollow bamboo, converted into a sort of blow-pipe and worked by the mouth. These so-called Malays must have been some of them local Malay debt-bondsmen and others slaves proper, pagan Mandailings and Rawas from the Batak tribes of Sumatra, whose earnings went to their masters. Even in this century washing for tin out of river-sand has been a favourite occupation for Mandailing and Rawa women in Kinta, their connection with the locality having arisen possibly from ancestors imported as slaves. It was not till the 19th century that the Chinese came to dominate the industry. In 1886 there were 350 private Malay mines in Kinta alone. Directly and indirectly the tin required first for bronze drums and axe-heads, then for Indian images, then for European pewter and finally for motor cars and canning must have brought the Malay down the centuries something more than the bare subsistence provided by fishing and gardening. To-day the industry is mechanised and benefits mostly the Chinese and British shareholder. Yet even in the old days the bulk of the profits went to those contemporary capitalists, the Malay ruler and chiefs, while under British administration royalty on tin at least provided the humblest with great social services.

So much for Malay industries. But how was Malay produce marketed? Originally there would have been only barter. Then the Indo-Chinese or Hindu introduced a currency; in old Malacca and elsewhere, there were tiny gold coins, but clumsy tin pieces were the commonest form. Money in any shape meant a great advance in economic and social life, though it added more debtors to the ranks of slaves. Always big transactions were kept in the hands of Hinduized rulers and chiefs, who could reckon in larger sums. Only small trading was left for peasants trafficking in boats and women selling food stuffs in evening markets.

There were no middle-class specialists in distribution until lately in the fishing industry.

Among primitive Indonesians a chief led his people in commerce as well as in the judicial court and on the battlefield, a practice intelligible enough when property belonged as much to the tribe as to the individual. "Batak rajas are often as poor as the poorest villagers though they have bigger and better houses. Only a few are rich and this is through trade, which is conducted almost entirely by the Rajas." These words apply equally to the position in Malaya before the entry of the British into the States; for it had been easy to graft the Hindu custom of royal trading on to the primitive Malay practice. In mediaeval Malacca, we are told by Tomé Pires, Sultan Muzaffar Shah "bought and built junks and sent them out with merchants", and again that the kings of Malacca were very rich because they got large profits from having a share of the cargo in every junk that left the port. The "Malay Annals" relate of the Bendahara Sri Maharaja Mutahir that he was richer than the wealthiest Tamil merchant in Malacca, that his ventures never failed, that he had so many slaves he could not recognize them all and that he thought nothing of giving his grand-children handfuls of gold-dust to play with. Pires talks of this Bendahara's great jewels and five quintals of gold. In 1641 the Dagh-Register relates how the Sultan of Kedah traded with Bengal and had just sold the Dutch tin and four elephants which he had bought from Tamils. In the next year His Highness sent so much tin to Coromandel in his royal vessels that the Dutch had no chance of getting half Kedah's annual output as the Sultan had promised. In the same year a new Sultan of Kedah himself sailed to Coromandel with seven elephants and 200 *bahar* of tin, just as the early rulers of Malacca had traded to China. In 1665 Mr. Lock, an English free trader in Kedah, sailed to Coromandel with two yachts, one on his own account and one on the Sultan's behalf, taking twenty elephants. By 1670 the king of Kedah and his nobles owed the Dutch Company f.55784.8.8. In Perak at that time credit dealings were forbidden except for small quantities of piece-goods and calicoes supplied to the Sultan and nobles on their written application. Captain Alexander Hamilton has described how a younger brother of Sultan 'Abd al-Jalil Shah of Johor, moving in 1708 to Riau, caused a rebellion to break out there four years later by his tyranny in "engrossing all trade in his own hands, buying and selling at his own prices". During the 18th century the Bugis rajas who gained the throne of Selangor, the second office in the Riau-Lingga empire and influence in Kedah, Perak and Sungai Ujong, were as energetic in commerce as in political intrigue. In 1771 Francis Light recorded that at that time Malay princes were always the principal merchants. It is amusing, therefore, to hear of Sultan Husain of Singapore and Temenggong 'Abd al-Rahman laughing at Raffles' offer to get them goods from Bengal to sell on commission, as trade was not for men of their standing. 'Abd al-Rahman's son, Temenggong Daing Ibrahim, made a fortune out of a boom in gutta-percha. In 1848 the Singapore Chamber of Commerce complained that this Temenggong had monopolised the trade, which was valued at more than $150,000 a year. His armed followers intercepted Malay boats bringing gutta-percha for sale to Singapore, till in defiance of all opposition he secured about nine-tenths of the produce, "whence it was inferred that extreme influence of some kind was used or some part of it would have found its way to parties who offered much higher prices".

Then there was the petty trade of small people. Tomé Pires tells how "ordinary" Malays "came to trade in Malacca in small boats (*prahu*). They bring *timah* (tin) and rice, chickens, goats, pigs, sugar-cane, *oraquas* (areca-nuts) and things like that." Whether their own Malay rulers or the Portuguese or the Dutch were in power, these poor wretches were subject to tax and toll. Nor did taxes go to build roads. In Newbold's time, the Jempul Malays had to take their produce an eight days' journey down-river to Malacca or convey it overland to Pahang.

Tomé Pires relates how in the 16th century "Malacca had so much a month from the women street-sellers, and this was given to the mandarins. . . . In Malacca they sell in every street. And as a great favour an inhabitant was allowed to have in front of his door a stall for selling and hiring. They also pay dues on the fruit and fish: this was a trifle."

On his trip to Trengganu and Kelantan in 1830 Munshi 'Abdullah saw women hawkers bring their garden produce in baskets on their heads to a market that was always held from sunset to nightfall. Such markets are common in Java and among the Minangkabaus. In the peninsula they lapsed, possibly owing to anarchy, the presence of many foreigners and British bye-laws for towns.

What effect then did British protection have on the Malay economy? Down to 1941 the British gave the agriculturist and fisherman peace for their labours. The abolition of the sumptuary laws of Hinduized courts made it possible for the Malay to own a good house, have well-stocked rice-barns and buy jewellery for his women-folk without fear of confiscation. Under British administration he was forbidden by law to indulge in the cock-fighting and gambling that had wasted his substance, and in the opium that had wasted his body. Instead, a new source of revenue was found in land-rents that caused the Malay to value and care for his garden and rice-fields as never before, the British introduction of security of tenure quickly raising the price of an *orlong* of rice-land in Krian from $10 to $60 or $70. Then, while in 1830 Munshi 'Abdullah found a large ox in Kelantan fetching $2 to $3 only, a large goat $1 and a cow buffalo $2 to $2.50, British steamships, roads and railways have enabled produce and cattle to be transported to open and profitable markets. For, after centuries of monopoly, British free trade gave the Malay a competitive price for the produce of his fish-traps and his fields and plantations. British science, too, introducing new forms of cultivation, especially rubber that requires no large capital expenditure, brought

In the Market, Kuala Trengganu

[*face p. 134*

him the novelty of an income so far above his daily needs that he could build a substantial house and buy cycles and gramophones and cars. British education enabled him to keep accounts and to correspond with foreign buyers.

So much to the credit of British influence on Malay material civilisation. On the debit side are the flooding of Malaya with foreign machine-made goods that have extinguished native arts and crafts, the attraction exercised by British rule for Indian and Chinese immigrants as many as the total Malay population, and the introduction of an industrial and capitalist system alien to Malay experience. In the face of these three innovations the Malay has lagged behind European, Indian and Chinese. The main reasons for this are not the laziness of which he is too readily accused but a failure to specialize and a failure to acquire and realize the importance of capital. The Malay, it is true, may in the eyes of the materialist waste time over such observances as the ritual of the rice-field as the Christian may waste time over a service of intercession. But the Malay agriculturist has no workless Sunday; his weddings are celebrated in the slack season after harvest, and his Muslim feast-days take the place of Europe's Christmas, Easter and bank holidays. What really excited Victorian criticism was the Malay attitude that, though a necessity, work cannot be counted a virtue. What the European moralist regards as lost time, the Malay regards as time gained.

The Malay failure to specialize was due firstly to his isolation in village communities encircled by forest and too small to maintain the specialist, and secondly it was due to bountiful nature that made livelihood easy. The pirate, the fisherman, the blacksmith, the carpenter, the weaver, the medicine-man were also rice-planters in season. Only the luxury demands of the few courts encouraged a more complete specialization in weaving, metal-work and the forging of weapons, crafts that became obsolete or waned before foreign competition. And being generally no specialist the Malay was supplanted by those who were, by the Chinese carpenter, miner and merchant, by the Indian cook, laundry-man and clerk, by the British doctor and planter, by the Japanese weaver and deep-sea fisherman. In 1938, out of Singapore's 11,500 tons of fresh fish 46 per cent. was got by a few Japanese fleets equipped with ice storage, and that in spite of the great preponderance of Malay (and Chinese) fishermen. Even more impressive are comparative statistics collected by Professor Raymond Firth. "While the Malay fishermen on the coast of Kelantan had an output of roughly $1\frac{1}{2}$ tons of fish a head *per annum*, the Japanese bream fishermen and drift-netters at the height of their prosperity (from 1926-1933) were producing about 8.3 tons, and the Chinese ring-net mackerel fishers of Pangkor (in 1938) about 10 tons. These figures may be compared with those of British fisheries, which before the war employed about 80,000 men and landed about 1,000,000 tons of fish *per annum*. Thus the average output of the British fisherman is about six or eight times that of the average Malayan fisherman." It is satisfactory to know that the government is now paying more attention to the development of Malay fisheries.

The Malay fishing industry illustrates the Malay's omission to accumulate capital as well as his omission to specialize. In south Trengganu and north Pahang and on the west coast the owner of the boat net or trap operated by the Malay may be a Chinese fish-dealer, who in return enjoys a monopoly of the catches at a low price, thus depriving the Malay of proper remuneration for his labour. For failure on the part of the Malay to save his own capital there are three historical reasons. Accumulation of capital was impossible under the tribal system with its communist propensities. At Jasin in the 1890's Dr. Blagden was pressed to fine those who charged fellow villagers more than 3 cents a *gantang* for *padi*, more than 10 cents a *gantang* for husked rice, more than $2\frac{1}{2}$ cents for two pieces of palm-sugar, more than 1 cent for a coconut, more than $\frac{1}{2}$ a cent for a duck's egg and a $\frac{1}{4}$ cent for a hen's egg. To demand more than these customary prices was to invite bad harvests. For under the matrilineal tribal system the high water-mark of wealth was not that of the individual but that of the tribe. The second historical reason operated as we have seen in the Hinduized patriarchal states, where to accumulate possessions was to invite the greedy attention of chiefs, with consequent confiscation and punishment. As for the chiefs themselves, when they waxed rich, life offered so few opportunities for enterprise or extravagance, that their gold could only be converted into jewellery. In more recent times, when a Malay did make money out of tin or rubber and had some notion of investment, the Muslim law against taking interest also militated against a modern use of capital. Now one of these obstacles has been abolished and the other two are yielding before modernism. Ancient custom even, as our review of Malay law has shown, always refused to recognize certain practices dating back to Hindu times as usurious. Professor Raymond Firth has collected notable instances from Kelantan. If a Kelantan rice-planter borrows money on the security of his land, the creditor will take half the crops as interest (and not as instalments of repayment), until the loan has been repaid in full. Or a rice-planter may borrow and agree that for every ten dollars received he will hand over ten *gantang* of rice at every harvest, again as interest only. A Malay may lend money to a coconut planter, when as interest he will take until the loan has been repaid all the produce less the small cost of plucking. If a Kelantan fisherman borrows money for a wedding on the security of a boat or borrows money to buy a boat, the lender again takes as interest a half or in some places a third share of the fish caught. This Malay system of interest has one advantage that, if there is a bad fishing season or a poor harvest, interest lessens automatically and does not accumulate, a circumstance that in Malay eyes makes it lawful under his religion.

The prime difficulty of the Malay to-day is how to acquire capital to apply to industry. A government scholarship can qualify him to be civil servant, doctor, lawyer. If he wants to enter commerce, he finds that Chinese and Indians reserve employment for their own races. Should he venture to start a business on his own, not only does he lack the international contacts Chinese and Indian commerce has established for centuries, but he has to face the active opposition of those sojourners in his native land. A Kelantan Malay tried to start a firm for the purchase of rice from his own countrymen, whereupon the Chinese hauliers raised the hire of lorries for this interloper so that he could not compete with Chinese buyers. A Malay co-operative society attempted to sell copra direct to Singapore, but as the only carriers were a Chinese shipping line, the first cargo was left on the jetty and the next arrived short in weight, wily sailors having pushed part of it overboard. The Kedah government when calling for tenders for building once laid it down as a condition that a proportion of the labour employed must be Malay, with the result that no Chinese or Indian contractor tendered. Equipped as fitters at a government artizans' school (and excellent fitters Malays are) two Malays got jobs with a municipality, whereupon the Indian foreman set them at once to mend foul night-soil carts in the hope of ejecting them from an Indian preserve. Poverty and persecution lead to revolt, whether it takes the form of communism or rabid nationalism, and the problem of the near future will be to find an entry into commerce for the Malay, without which his race must feel more and more discontent and resentment.

Note.—Before 1511 Malacca was the entrepot for pepper from Perak, Kedah and north Sumatra. Kelantan also produced pepper. The Lusiads and Barbosa both mention the importance of Kedah pepper. In 1670 Acheh destroyed its plantations to secure its own monopoly of the trade with Europe and China. But references to the Kedah pepper trade continue. In 1790 Francis Light helped a Chinese to open 400 acres for pepper on Penang and by 1803 the island produced 4 million pounds. The Napoleonic war nearly killed the trade. And though it recovered, falling prices made it impossible for Penang and Malacca to compete with independent producers in Trengganu, Sumatra, Borneo and Siam. *The Changing Balance of the early South-East Asia pepper trade.* John Bastin, Kuala Lumpur, 1960.

8: LITERATURE

For a thousand years the Malay was under the influence of Hinduized courts, that were centres of Buddhism and Saivism, Hindu magical science, Hindu art and literature. During that time he borrowed two Indian scripts, the Pallavan from which Java as early as the 8th century A.D. evolved its *kawi* alphabet, and the *nagari* script brought in the 8th century by the Palas from Bengal. A guild of Tamil traders in the same century left scraps of their Buddhist story of Manimekalai in Sumatran folk-tales that have been re-told in the Malay peninsula and written down in modern times.

Of Malay literature in Indian scripts nothing remains. There are indeed a few inscriptions but the only one of literary interest is an epitaph of A.D. 1380 on the tombstone of a Pasai princess, that in characters akin to those on inscriptions of the Sumatran king Adityavarman (1340–75) gives us in a mixture of Malay Sanskrit and Arabic an example of Malay verse in a Sanskrit metre. To the same century belongs the inscription on a Trengganu stele recording in the same mixed vocabulary Islamic penalties for sexual offences, the carved characters being the first known example of the Malayo-Arabic script.

The literature proper of the Malay's Hindu period has survived only in manuscripts written in this Perso-Arabic alphabet (that is still employed) and in language already marked by a large sprinkling of Arabic loan-words. The Malay language of prehistoric times had a precise vocabulary of concrete terms, but until it had borrowed from Sanskrit words like *price, property, soul, work, time, punishment, religion* and *fasting*, it was destitute of words to express social, ethical, religious and other abstract ideas. Sanskrit came to the Malays through Indians conversant with magic and the ritual of their religions, immigrants too few to introduce Prakrit, its colloquial form. The last Indian influence came from the south, introducing many Sanskrit words in Tamil form and, later, Persian and Arabic words that Islam had carried to India. This is Malay as we know it, though many religious terms were imported afterwards by missionaries from the Hadramaut, and a sprinkling of culture words was borrowed from Portuguese, Dutch and English, while nowadays politics are introducing many words from Batavian Malay.

In the Hindu period the Indian epics were popularized in Java and in the Majapahit colonies of Malaya more by the shadow-play than by written translations. So popular were they that scenes from the Ramayana were carved early in the 10th century on a Prambanan temple and again four centuries later at Chandi Panataran. In the 15th century when *kawi* was no longer understood, fresh versions of the Ramayana were written in New Javanese, and it is to them and to the popular dramatic version of Jokya that the Malay texts are related. All those texts appear to come from a source into which had flowed flotsam and jetsam from the east, south and south-west of India, and various incidents in the story attest the arrival of Indian elements after the 12th century. Non-Indian elements are few and have not marred the sequence of the original epic. The oldest manuscript of the Ramayana, or as Malays call it, the *Hikayat Sri Rama*, reached the Bodleian library from the collection of Archbishop Laud in 1633, but it happens to be a late text with a Muslim colouring. An unpublished MS. in the library of the Royal Asiatic Society, London, contains an episode reminiscent of Odysseus' stratagem with the rams of Polyphemus; Dasarata hiding sixty warriors under goats that butt and kill Ravana's warriors.

The Malay versions of the Bharatayuddha (a section of the Mahabharata) and of the story of Bhauma, son of Bhumi the Earth, are named respectively the *Hikayat Perang Pandawa Jaya* and the *Hikayat Sang Boma* (or *Samba*). Unlike the Malay texts of the Ramayana, both are derived from originals in *kawi*, the old Javanese alphabet that expired about 1400. In the story of the war of the Victorious Pandavas, the Malay enjoyed for once the fleeting loveliness that Java borrowed from the Hindus and crystallized in the sculpture of Bara-budur and Prambanan. Take, for example, Krishna's first glimpse of the City of Elephants:—

> He saw Hastina-pura, dim as a woman covered with rice-powder and peering from behind a door. The jewelled roof of the palace glittered like the rays of the sun. Trees swayed in the wind like people waving to him. Beasts gave cries of welcome. Bulbuls murmured as if they were asking after Arjuna. All the fish in the ponds swam to the surface to escort him, darting and dancing under the water-lilies or sheltering under the lotus-blooms as under coloured umbrellas.

The spirit of delight that animates such passages came from Hindu India and with sculpture and art was doomed to fall before Islam as Hastina-pura fell before the Pandavas.

An example of the wide-spread influence of the Hindu epics on Malay literature is a passage that occurs in the Mahabharata and other works of ancient India, in the *kawi* version of the Bharatayuddha done in A.D. 1157, in the Malay *Hikayat Raja-Raja Pasai*, the *Sejarah Melayu*, the *Hikayat Hang Tuah* and many Malay folk-tales and romances:—

> The women hurried to see Krishna (approaching Hastina-pura); some with hair dishevelled and untied, others with disordered dress, others with face half powdered, some with quids of tobacco (*bersisēk*) half prepared, some with only one eye painted. All the shopkeepers left their wares, and salesmen stopped in the midst of selling, exclaiming, "We don't care if our goods are stolen, provided we see Krishna". Some had oil only on one side of their heads and powder only on one side of their bodies. Wives left husbands and children, while some held up their breasts and cried, "We present these (*susu-ku ini akan haluan aku*) to Batara Krishna". All the women of Hastina-pura hurried as if they were being chased by an enemy and some brought dolls (*anak-*

anakan) saying, "There is your father Batara Krishna". They rushed to climb platforms and the platforms collapsed and they fell sprawling, some with broken limbs, others with limbs sprained or bruised.

Their versions of the Hindu epics thrown on the screen made the Malays quick to follow a plot, and though the shadow-play left the characters hardly more than puppets, so popular were performances of the Ramayana that Muslim frowns failed to ban them and only now are they dying out before the cinema. But India's impression on Malay life still survives in beast stories derived from the Panchatantra, the Katha Sarit Sagara or Ocean of Story and especially the Buddhist Jataka tales.

Another pre-Islamic element in Malay literature is the Javanese cycle of Panji tales that date from the second half of the 14th century, when knowledge of Sanskrit and *kawi* had waned and the Indian metres of Old Javanese works were no longer found and Middle Javanese based on popular speech had started. Many Panji tales were translated into Malay in mediaeval Malacca, in Kelantan and elsewhere, and all but one of the peninsular manuscripts await study. Like the Hindu epics the tales were popularized by the shadow-play, and some have thought that their wide diffusion was due to imperial propaganda by Majapahit, which in the 14th century conquered Malaya. The oldest version, the *Hikayat Galuh di-gantong* comes from Palembang, and one of its characters is a nun, Panji's aunt, whose mountain haunt was Gunong Puchangan or in the Cambodian version Phnom-pachangan. The forms of personal names suggest that it was from Malay versions that the Panji cycle reached Cambodia and Siam. For though the cycle has a common kernel, there are many variations of the main theme. In early versions (like Kelantan's *Kuda Sumirang Sri Panji Pandai Rupa*) Panji's first love is Martalangu a goddess incarnate as the daughter of a headman and therefore murdered by the hero's mother for her lowly birth. But in the Malay Panji poem, *Ken Tambuhan*, she is a princess of

Daha, for whose murder there is no reason, so that she has to be restored to life. Like Malay annalists, the authors of the Panji cycle have used stuff from old popular tales; history and geography being employed as wildly as in Malay folk-lore. And although the cycle is Javanese, the tales include indiscriminate borrowings from the Ramayana, the Mahabharata, the Sudamala and the folk-lore of the Deccan, that was soon to flood the Malay region with romances made up of Hindu and Muslim ingredients. Of one tale, called *Chĕkĕl Waneng Pati* after one of Panji's many aliases, van der Tuuk wrote: "It is one of the most interesting Malay compositions and has influenced almost every literary production in Malay." The buffoon and cowardly braggart of Malay folk romances, the ennobling of animals with grandiloquent Sanskrit titles in the *Hikayat Pelandok Jinaka*, the preposterous demands of the fairy princess of Gunong Ledang in the "Malay Annals", the story of Chandra Kirana and Sultan Mansur in the same annals, the riddles of Malay folk-tales, the Tamil appendix following the Javanese nucleus of the *Hikayat Hang Tuah*—all these find sources in this Panji tale. In fact the *Hikayat Hang Tuah*, the only original Malay romance till lately, is modelled upon the Panji tales and is full of the incidents of Javanese romance. It is difficult for the modern town Malay accustomed to the cinema to understand the appeal this Javanese cycle had for his ancestors. The tales are devoid of psychological depth or moral purport, but they are tales of adventure, and the puppets of the shadow-play had so great an aesthetic attraction, that many of the tales are still performed in the shadow-plays of villages in northern Malaya. It is the irony of fate that while the good they did has passed, the evil in them survived. For while translation from Javanese, a language akin to Malay, did no damage to Malay literary style but rather enlarged its scope, the influence of the Panji tales as of the shadow-play romances was otherwise malign, encouraging Malay writers to be content with noble puppets, sumptuous repasts and gilded equipages instead of delineating men and women "not too bright and good for human nature's daily food".

Shortly after A.D. 1400 Malacca embraced Islam, to be followed by the rest of Malaya, by the coastal peoples of Sumatra, Borneo and Celebes and by Java. With this change of religion the Malay world became flooded by romances from the Deccan that, still full of Hindu mythology and tags from the Panji tales, were compact of the Hinduized folk-lore of Muslim India, reminiscences from Persian tales like the story of Amir Hamza, allusions to the heroes of the Shah-Namah like Kobad, Jamshid and Bahram, incidents from the Alexander legend, references to Baghdad, Madinah, Egypt and Byzantium and even expositions of Sufi mysticism. Such a hotchpotch of Hindu epics, Javanese tales and Tamil folk-lore was to be expected from a cosmopolitan port like the Malacca of the 15th century. And the composite nature of every Malay romance is illustrated by the recurrent use of that common Indian *motif*, the search for an object to cure illness or barrenness. The hero of the popular *Hikayat Indra Bangsawan* is a perfect paladin of folk-lore, rescuer of a princess from a land ravaged by Vishnu's Garuda, owner of a magic suit that changes him to any shape, a knight errant in quest of a bamboo musical instrument that will give him a kingdom and of tigress' milk to cure the eyes of his mistress. He offers to give tigress' milk to any of her nine princely suitors who will have his thigh branded, brands them all and gives them goats' milk. The association of branding with the quest for medicine makes the tale akin to the Gul Bakawali, a compilation of 1702 by Nipal Chand, that was done into Malay in 1875 from the Hindustani. Another romance, the *Hikayat Nakhoda Muda*,[1] is interesting because it contains a plot used by Shakespeare. The gist of it occurs in the 11th century "Ocean of Story". It is the plot of "All's Well that Ends Well":—

> When thou canst get the ring upon my finger which never shall come off, and show me a child begotten of thy body that I am father to, then call me husband; but in such a "then" I write a "never".

[1] The gist of a variant version, *Ht. Maharaja Bikrama Sakti*, was known to Voltaire (Zadig, ch. 3).

In the Malay version there is propounded a riddle that occurs in a modern Greek tale. In a passage in another romance, the *Hikayat Indraputra*, as well as in a parody of it in the *Hikayat Pelandok Jinaka*, there is the literary device of iterated enquiry as to the identity of persons passing in procession that is employed in the third book of the Iliad. Malay romances may have adventitious interest of this kind but all are marked by the faults of Sidney's "Arcadia", as Virginia Woolf described them. "Telling stories, Sidney thought, was enough—one could follow another interminably. But where there is no end in view, there is no sense of direction to draw us on. Nor, since it is part of his scheme to keep his characters simply bad and simply good without distinction, can he gain variety from the complexity of character. To supply chance and movement, he must have recourse to mystification. These changes of dress, these disguises of princes as peasants, of men as women serve instead of psychological subtlety to relieve the stagnancy of people collected together with nothing to talk about. But when the charm of that childish device falls flat, there is no breath left to fill his sails. Who is talking and to whom and about what we no longer feel sure."

A Muslim colour was given to these romances, partly to save them from the Muslim index, partly to employ them —the *Hikayat Shah-i Mardan*, for example—as propaganda for the new faith. But the first task of the missionaries was to substitute for the Hindu epics tales of the heroes of Islam, like Alexander the Great, Amir Hamza and Muhammad Hanafiah. The stories of those heroes were translated into Malay from the Persian at least as early as the 15th century. No wonder that in spite of its inordinate length and the iteration of its missionary purpose, a romance like that of Alexander could hold Malays spell-bound. The valley of ants, the giraffe-riders, the cave-dwellers with one foot and one eye; the place where angels told their beads above the sun and the noise of that luminary's descent made Alexander faint; the great flies that stoned his troops and were only driven away when one of their number was caught saddled and mounted by a puppet rider; the angels, who pierced with lances the devils that dwelt in Coptic idols; the bird-worshipping Circassians in tiger-skin tunics; the nude gymnosophists who marvelled that a mortal should bother to subdue a world; Gog and Magog; the diamond mines of Ophir and the copper walls of Jabalqa; the riding on mares into the land of darkness and the visit to the spring of life—these and other episodes provided the Malay with what Europe found in the Odyssey, Marco Polo, Robinson Crusoe and Jules Verne. A touch of the spiritual, delineation of character beneath the gold and the silk, and individuality of style, these could have turned the stories of Alexander and Tamim al-Dari into Odysseys and made them works of great art.

The Muslim legends known to the Malay have been divided into:—

(a) romances of pre-Islamic heroes like Alexander, Nabi Yusuf (or Joseph of the Old Testament), Nabi Isa or Jesus, the Persian hero, Amir Hamza, and the Arabian, Saif Dhu'l-Yazan;

(b) stories of the Prophet, the earlier ones from the Persian, and stories of the Shiah saints, Hasan and Husain, and Muhammad Hanafiah;

(c) the adventures of people about the Prophet, fantastic and devoid of historical and geographical similitude, like the tale of Tamim al-Dari, and

(d) locally concocted tales like the *Hikayat Raja Handak* or *Raja Lahad*, where ignorance of Arabic has led to the fabrication of heroes out of words that mean respectively a "moat" and a "place".

Besides these works, Islam introduced the Malays to three cycles of tales of world-wide fame. There is the excellent

Malay version of the "Tales of a Parrot" (the Sanskrit *Sukasaptati* and Persian *Tuti-nameh*): three times in the text the work is ascribed to one, Kadli Hasan, and twice a date, A.D. 1371, is given. The 15th century "Malay Annals" mention a daughter of a Laksamana of Malacca, Khoja Hasan, who was named Sabariah, almost certainly after the heroine of one of these tales. The Malay version, called *Hikayat Bayan Budiman*, must have come from some early Persian recension. Another cycle is the *Kalila dan Damina*, derived ultimately from the *Panchatantra* or Five Moral Tales compiled in Kashmir about A.D. 300 and best known in Europe as the Fables of Bidpai. This collection of fables reached the Malay archipelago at different times and in different ways. One of the tales is illustrated on the 9th century Chandi Mendut in Java and the frame-work of the book on the 13th century Chandi Jago. There are three Javanese and two Madurese versions. In Malay there are three recensions: one translated from some South Indian source between 1504 and 1726, another entirely different translated by Munshi 'Abdullah from Tamil in 1835, and a third from a Dutch translation and a French version of the Turkish recension, Humayun-Nameh. The oldest version, to judge from the printed text, was done by some clever foreigner or half-caste in the Dutch Indies who had not mastered Malay syntax and idiom, but a better edition based on comparative study of MSS. is wanted. Of the third or Bakhtiar cycle the Malay has two main recensions: (1) the early *Hikayat Puspa Wiraja*, done from a non-Muslim Indian source probably in mediaeval Malacca, and (2) the *Hikayat Golam* and the last part of the 17th century *Hikayat Kalila dan Damina*, the latter from a late Persian adaptation and the former third-hand through two Arabic adaptations of the original Persian text. Allied to the *Hikayat Puspa Wiraja* are two small Muslim redactions, the *Hikayat Bakhtiar* and the *Hikayat Maharaja 'Ali*, neither of which has more than a faint resemblance to the Persian recension. Though ultimately from the Persian, the *Hikayat Golam* or *Hikayat Azbakh* or *Hikayat Zadah Bokhtin*, as it is variously named, exhibits strong Arabic colouring and was translated into Malay in the 17th century. One episode in it finds a parallel only in a Zanzibar MS. of the "Thousand and One Nights".

To European taste the tales in these three famous cycles will be among the more readable of Malay works.

Conversion to Islam brought a flood of Malay translations of works on Muslim jurisprudence, dogma and mysticism. One of the earliest, a good book of morality, is an unidiomatic rendering from the Persian, done in 1603 and entitled *Taj al-Salatin*. It is a miscellany tinged with pantheism and dealing with the nature of man, God and the world, with death, with the early Caliphs and their honourable poverty, with just and unjust rulers and officials, with intelligence and the science of physiognomy. More scholarly are the pantheist works in Arabic and in Malay of Shams al-din of Pasai (d. 1630), for whom only God is real and man a puppet in His shadow-play (p. 39). A famous contemporary of Shams al-din at Acheh was another Sumatran, Hamzah of Barus, whose metaphysical verse makes him incomparably the greatest literary figure among Malay religious writers. One of Hamzah's prose passages contains a simile found in the Katha Upanishad, in St. Augustine and the Fathers, and repeated in Lyly's Euphues, by Francis Bacon, Milton and Sidney Smith. It runs as follows: "A man asks, 'If God is immanent in the world, is He immanent in filth'? The answer is that the heat of the sun is for all the world, for the foul and for the clean, for the Ka'abah and for the heathen temple. It falls on the foul and is not defiled, on the clean and is not cleansed, on the evil and is not corrupted; from the K'abah it derives no benefit, from the heathen temple no harm. If that is so with the sun, how can Almighty God, the purest of the pure, be defiled or corrupted?" A stern critic of the heterodox views of the two Sumatran pantheists was Shaikh Nur al-din bin 'Ali al-Raniri, son of a Gujerati by a Malay mother, a prolific author, who settled in Acheh and wrote a well-known book on the pillars of Islam called *Sirat al-mustakim* and a scholarly history entitled *Bustan al-Salatin* "The Garden of Kings" with a conclusion on science, including physiognomy and medicine. He wrote also many polemical treatises, comparing Hamzah's pantheism with the nihilistic theories of the Vedantas and the Mahayana Buddhism of Tibet. In spite of a mediaeval cosmogony and neo-Platonic absurdities, Nur al-din was highly educated and is one of the most distinguished thinkers who wrote in Malay.

An interesting work on Islam in the middle ages is the *Kitab Sa-ribu Masa'alah* or "Book of the thousand question", of which one copy has been printed at Mecca, and another at Singapore by Malay editors from Trengganu and Kelantan. The existence in Malay of the fullest version of the first Arabic account of Islam that Europe got to know brings home to us vividly that Malay was one of the languages of Muslim culture. The work was written in Arabic as early as A.D. 963 and was translated into Latin at Toledo after 1085 when the Moors lost Spain for ever. Persian, Portuguese, Dutch and Javanese translations exist. In the Malay version there is reference to so many place-names round the Caspian sea that it has been surmised the original author may have lived at Bokhara. The Malay translator has followed two early Persian texts. The hero of the book is a half historical half legendary Rabbi. The Traditions say that this Jew went to Medinah and put Muhammad three questions that only a Prophet could answer. Proving by hard questions was a test applied by the Queen of Sheba to Solomon and by Bedouins as well as Jews to Muhammad; and critics have detected a resemblance between this half legendary Rabbi, 'Abdu'llah ibn Salam, and Nicodemus. Some of the questions put by him are inspired by the Taurat or Jewish scriptures. The answers given by the Prophet employ the usual properties of the Muslim cosmogony. There is a picture of Anti-Christ entering Isfahan on a donkey so large that the deepest sea wetted only his fetlocks. The Angel of Death kills himself at Allah's command, groaning and remorseful like some wicked giant in a fairy tale, while the tortures of the damned are portrayed with the imagination of Hieronymus Bosch. Mountains are described as the nails of the universe, which indeed must need them, as it is balanced on the horns of a bull, who is kept quiet for fear of a mosquito bigger than an elephant that stings his nostril if he thinks of shaking his head. One of the questions asked is "Why cannot one be two and two be three and so on?" The Prophet replies that one is one because Allah is one; and two cannot be three because God created Adam and Eve, day and night, height and depth; and three cannot be four because God is three with Adam and Muhammad and God instituted three stages for Muslim divorce; and four cannot be five because Allah inspired the Old Testament, the Psalms, the Kuran and the Gospels. In paradise virgin houris spring out of the pods of the trees, and some of the herbage is camphor grass from Barus in Sumatra. Such ideas are as far from the educated Malay of to-day as from the sophisticated European.

The finest literary work in the Malay language is a 15th century history, the *Sejarah Melayu* or "Malay Annals", written by an author whose vivid account of life in mediaeval Malacca shows that he was there before it was captured by d'Albuqerque in 1511, and (unless there have been interpolations) lived long enough to embroider his narrative with a story of the amazement of the Malays at Portuguese bullets, though in 1511 they themselves possessed cannon. Until recently it was wrongly thought that these annals were compiled at Pasai or in Johor in 1612; the original apparently having been carried to Goa by the Portuguese, when they sacked Johor Lama in 1536, and not recovered till the later date. The author's cosmopolitan culture, only to be acquired in a centre like Malacca, includes a smattering of Chinese, Siamese and Portuguese. Sanskrit and Persian and Tamil words, Javanese sentences and Arabic texts, the Ramayana and the Bhagavad Gita and the cycle of Panji tales are all familiar to him. He records how a mountain princess refused the hand of a Malacca Sultan until he should bring her seven trays of lices' livers, a tub of tears, a tub of the juice of young betel palms, a basin of his own blood and a basin of his son's blood. In the Persian Sindi-bad Namah a merchant parts with sandalwood to a rogue, who persuaded him it was worthless, on condition that he is given in return "whatever else he may choose". Finding himself swindled, he resorts in disguise to the rogue's den and hears its blind chief rate his subordinate's folly:—"Instead of asking for gold, this merchant may require you to give him a measure of male fleas with silken housings and jewelled trapping, and how will you do that?" The annalist makes Malay rajas write letters to their adversaries before engaging in battle, as Alexander does at the prompting of Nabi Khadir in the *Hikayat Iskandar*. He has borrowed long passages from that romance and from the oldest of Malay histories, the "Chronicles of Pasai". In addition he has imitated the style and method of the Pasai history. Both chroniclers invent fantastic origins for place-names like Pasai and Malacca. The downfall of a handsome young warrior at Pasai is copied in the adventures of Hang Tuah and Hang Kesturi at Malacca. So, too, the mythical account of the conversion of a Pasai ruler to Islam is copied in the "Malay Annals" and, later, in the "Kedah Annals". Finally both in the Pasai chronicle and in the "Malay Annals" long ethical exhortations are put into the mouths of dying Sultans.

Other peninsular histories include the *Misa Melayu*, an attractive contemporary account of Perak between 1742 and 1778; a romantic hotchpotch the "Kedah Annals" or *Hikayat Merang Mahawangsa*, built up of local folk-lore and myth from the Ramayana, the Jataka tales and the *Hikayat Amir Hamza;* and an anonymous history of Johor between 1672 and the last decade of the 18th century. The last considerable Malay historian was Raja 'Ali Haji bin Raja Ahmad, of Riau, who wrote *Silsilah Melayu dan Bugis* and in 1865 began his *Tuhfat al-Nafis*, the most important history after the *Sejarah Melayu;* both works deal with the Riau-Johor empire and the part the Bugis played in the Malaya of the 18th century.

A still more important figure was Munshi 'Abdu'llah bin 'Abdu'l-Kadir (1796–1854), son of a Malacca mother of

Indian descent and of a father with Arab and Tamil blood in his veins. He was the first Malay writer to depart from myth and legend and record contemporary events in a novel Autobiography, in an account of a Voyage to Kelantan and in another of his pilgrimage to Mecca on which he died. He is a master of a large vocabulary and an easy colloquial style, taking as his model the conversational passages in the "Malay Annals", but his Malay is not impeccable, being marred by foreign idioms. Only when one remembers the unintelligible translations from the English that now appear in the vernacular press can one fully appreciate his scholarship and the genuineness of his talent. His father was *munshi* to William Marsden and he himself to Sir Stamford Raffles, of whom he has left a vivid picture in his Autobiography; he also helped Newbold and Begbie in the writing of their books on Malaya.

The 19th century saw the last of the old type of romance in the *Hikayat Bestammam* and the *Hikayat Ganja Mara*. One of the century's few outstanding works was a translation (*Hikayat Penerang Hati*) of Aesop's Fables by a Perak Malay, Alang Ahmad bin Muhammad Yunus, later entitled Dato' Maha-Kurnia. Most Malay prose-writers were engaged in producing school primers.

The 20th century has been notable for the continued production of school books and for the development of Malay journalism and of works of fiction, some of them original, most of them translations. "Only contact with foreign literature and ability to appreciate it seem to be capable of giving the Malay the literary sense, the stimulus and the inspiration to write in his own language. Generally this has spoilt style, as more often than not thoughts are cast in the mould of the foreign model. And this failing seems to be more pronounced in the Malay's literary developments to-day than ever it was in a less complex age." That is the just verdict of Zain al-'abidin bin Ahmad, who under the pen-name of Zaba is himself perhaps the most distinguished of modern Malay writers. The first peninsular Malay to introduce the novel was Sayid Shaikh, a Malayo-Arab born in Malacca, who poured out fiction in order to pay for the publication of works on modern Islam, especially works from the pen of Shaikh Muhammad 'Abduh of the al-Azhar university at Cairo. Another Malay who has done much to translate and popularize the modern Arabic literature of Egypt is Ahmad Isma'il (b. 1899) of Kelantan. Many English books like "Gulliver's Travels", Lamb's "Tales from Shakespeare", Stevenson's "Treasure Island", and works by Ballantyne, Jules Verne, Rider Haggard and Edgar Wallace have been translated under the auspices of the Education Department. But contact with European influences has not so far inspired the Malay, as contact with the Hindu and the Javanese in mediaeval Malacca inspired him, or even as Arab and Egyptian literature has inspired him. Pantheism, which outside Catholicism has been called the religion of modern Europe, is within the range of Malay religious thought, but generally the Malay world is the theocentric world of the middle ages, hardly touched by the daring speculations of humanism in the realms of religion, ethics, psychology and physical science. It even took Japanese propaganda to destroy the divinity of Malay kings and inaugurate the era of the common man. The result of democracy on literature it is too early to foretell, but already politics have resulted in an inundation of Indonesian journalese, with foreign syntax and perpetual mistranslations, which damaging the Malay's implement for thought must also damage his intellectual life.

As of Malay prose so too there is a large body of Malay verse. Like Anglo-Saxon verse, the Malay's earliest essay in poetry is not metrical but consists of lines more or less uniform in length and with accents that occur with fair regularity. Padded with stock tags, this rugged rhythmical form survives in the incantations of the medicine-man, in the legal maxims and tribal songs of Negri Sembilan and in some rhapsodist tales. At least one of the tags in those tales is translated from the Tamil Manimekalai. Known by the Tamil name of *gurindam*, this rhythmical form goes back at least to the 14th or 15th century, when specimens of it are embodied in the prose of the *Hikayat Raja-Raja Pasai*. Some of the sayings of the Minangkabau tribes of Negri Sembilan rise to poetry by their heightened way of description:—

> Follow down the dragon's traces,
> And if thou wouldst find the hillocks,
> Islets footed in the marsh-land,
> Jungle fowl shall be thy leaders;
> Seekest thou the spreading meadow,
> By the grasshopper be guided;
> The spit of hills between the valleys
> By the bulbul shall be shown thee.[1]

Famous is a description of dawn from a folk version of the Ramayana:—

> Long had passed the hour of midnight;
> Twice ere now had infants wakened
> Truant youth were wending homeward;
> Elders turned about in slumber;
> Heavy dewdrops kept descending;
> Far away were pheasants calling;
> In forest depths the partridge fluted;
> Lowed the cattle in the meadows,
> Buffaloes from byres responded;
> Peacocks spread their tails at cock-crow;
> Up-rolled the curtain of the morning.
> Mag-pie robins 'gan to chirrup;
> Now aloft were night-jars soaring;
> Pigeons coo'ed upon the threshold,
> Fitful came the quail's low murmur;
> Foot-long brands had burned to inches.
> These the signs of day approaching.[2]

And here from the *Hikayat Awang Sulong* is a picture of a storm at sea.

> Wind searching as a sieve of brass,
> Laying all things flat before it,

[1] See Appendix A, p. 185.
[2] See Appendix A, p. 185.

> Driving clouds in pointed wisps,
> Like the trump on the day of judgment;
> Wind that's palpable in form,
> Tearing up the shrub in court-yard,
> From muddy soil the plants up-rooting,
> Tumbling buffalo in meadow,
> Toppling coconut in garden;
> Wind that strips the coral reef-banks,
> Till they show like slabs of metal;
> Tossing mullet on the deck-house,
> Bringing shark to door of cabin.[1]

Primitive though it is, this verse contains flotsam and jetsam from many sources. In *Malim Dēman* the Malay rhapsodist sings of:—

> Voices lifted high in singing,
> Till the apes fell from the branches;
> The flowing water stopped to listen,
> The flying bird turned back to hear.[2]

In his *Metamorphoses* (XIV, ii. 338–340) Ovid writes of the singing of Canens:—

> Et mulcere feras et flumina longa morari
> Ore suo volucresque vagas retinere solebat.

While on analogy rhythmical verse would appear its earliest form, the oldest Malay poetry, of which there is a dated record, is a type in a Sanskrit metre that occurs on a Pasai tombstone of A.D. 1380. It is not quite the metre for long Malay poems, like the *Kēn Tambuhan*, a Panji poem of the 15th century where the gods are still *dēwata mulia raya* and there is no mention of Allah or His Prophet. Individual quatrains retain the old Sanskrit name of *sloka*:—

> Hujan pun turun rintēk-rintēk bahasa,
> Tagar menderam di-angkasa,
> Merak berbunyi di-pohon rijaksa,
> Segala yang memandang belas-lah rasa.

[1] See Appendix A, p. 185.
[2] See Appendix A, p. 186.

Some of these poems are adaptations of Javanese romance, others of Indian romance. Well-known examples are the *Shaʻēr Si-lindong delima* alias *Sri Benian*, and the *Shaʻēr Bidasari*, two poems not far removed in plot. In the poem on Bidasari Vishnu's Garuda ravages Cambay and drives its king and queen into the forest, where the queen bears a daughter. Unable to carry the child on their flight, they leave her behind to be found by a merchant of Indrapura, whose daughter names her Bidasari. Jealous of her beauty and fearful lest the king marry her, the queen of Indrapura so persecutes Bidasari that her foster-father builds her a dwelling in the forest. There the king comes hunting and marries her. Finally her identity is revealed.

The end of the 16th century saw the composition of mystic religious poems by the Sumatran Hamzah of Barus. They are indebted to the erotic rhapsodies of Persian mystics and are too full of Arabic words to be intelligible to the average Malay, but at the same time they are sensuous and passionate:—

> When heat and cold have become the same,
> With greed and desire each an idle name,
> And your self's like wax resolved in the flame,
> Then smooth in the end you'll find life's game.[1]

There have been many verses written on religious and moral subjects since the time of Hamzah but none have had the fire and gusto of his pantheist verse.

Another class of *shaʻēr* is the topical like the verses describing a royal picnic in Perak's 18th century history, the *Misa Melayu*, or Munshi 'Abdullah's doggerel on a fire at Singapore or verses on the Perak war or verses on the eruption of Krakatau. Recent times have seen a crop of short poems, many erotic, others didactic and religious. Some of them are based on Persian models. An old poem with a metre of its own is a pretty but scandalous trifle, the *Shaʻēr Silambari*

[1] See Appendix A, p. 186.

or *Sha'ēr Sinyor Kosta*, which relates how a Portuguese abducted the Burmese mistress of a Chinese from Canton.

Most famous of all Malay verse-forms is the *pantun*, which has been developed from the Malay fondness for riddles that depend only on irrelevant sound suggestion for their point or simile. To take one example:—

> Sarang semut di-tanah gelap
> In cavern dark ants nest and bore

should prompt the reply

> Orang selimut lalu lelap
> In blanket stark you rest and snore.

And those who look for a meaning in the first half of every Malay quatrain should bear in mind that the challenging couplet in these jingling riddles is often nonsense. Malay-speaking Chinese improvise them, and it may not be mere coincidence that the elliptical art of the *pantun* is nearer to Chinese poetry than to any other. "In Chinese odes", Mr. Cranmer-Byng has told us, "before coming to the real object of the poem, in one or two lines a peculiar phenomenon, a well-known event or occurrence is mentioned as an introduction—not unlike a clever arabesque, in order to prepare reflection, sensation and the state of mind for what follows." And he translates an example, where allusions to blue-bottle flies in the first couplets put the hearer into a mood to appreciate the description in the second couplets of the way slander buzzes round a court and poisons palace life. That is the way the Chinese poet employs his eye for nature, and that is also the way of the Malay poet. "Dark is the cluster of sweet mangosteen fruit, while the creamy petals of a flower decay and fall. She may be dark but she is sweet to look at, and of what use is a creamy complexion that does not wear." Yet even when a first couplet is intended as an introduction to the second, the connection is often cryptic. There is a verse given in Marsden's "Malay Grammar":—

> Kerengga di-dalam buloh
>   Serahi berisi ayer mawar:
> Sampai hasrat di-dalam tuboh
>   Tuan sa-orang jadi penawar,

or, as Marsden translated it literally:

> Large ants in the bamboo-cane,
>   A flasket filled with rose-water;
> When the passion of love seizes my frame,
>   From you alone I can expect the cure.

Actually it is not nonsense but has a real meaning for the Malay or for anyone who has felt the bite of the red ant:—

> Red ants in a bamboo! the passion
>   That tortures my frame is like you:
> But like flask of rose-water in fashion
>   Is the cure my dear flame can bestow.

This convention of the *pantun* gives the observer of nature a wide scope, and the number of natural objects cited is abundant—swifts on the wing, the quail's cry, a scorpion on a sugar-cane, morning mist, dew on grass, a banyan tree beside a rice-plot, tall bamboo clumps, a pheasant's nest in a cleft above a water-fall, the splash of paddles, the sight of white paddles moving like the wings of white birds, convolvulus wreathing stalks in an abandoned rice-swamp, butterflies upon rocks by the sea, a monkey descending a tree to bathe in a moonlit marsh, the arched back of a leech, the praying mantis, tumbling dolphins, the sailing boat luffing past a sunken rock. Though this abundance of imagery is due partly to the compulsion of assonance and rhyme, it shows the Malay is not blind to nature, and it

LITERATURE 159

recalls the art of China more than any other. Here is one where assonance is joined with a relative simile:—

> From cotton coarse our thread we fashion,
> From the thread our fabric's wove.
> No remorse! When sped our passion,
> Count me dead and not your love.[1]

The effort to compete with the assonance contrived by the ingenious artifice of a rival singer will lead sometimes to far-fetched imagery and produce quatrains reminiscent of the limerick or Clerihew or even of Lewis Carroll's surrealist verse.

But far from being mere intellectual essays, the best *pantun* are "simple, sensuous and passionate". It is hard to translate verse so packed with meaning in a few words. Two examples recall Hazlitt's sensitive prose: "I never see a child's kite in the air, but it seems to pull at my heart. It is to me a thing of life. I feel the twinge at my elbow, the flutter and palpitation, with which I used to let go the string of my own, as it rose in the air and towered among the clouds. My little cargo of hopes and fears ascended with it."

> White as paper a-sail in the air
>   Are the kites of the boys on the quay;
> And I feel when in love with my fair,
>   Like a ship that is breasting the sea.

and

> Hard the divorce of love and lingering
>   Like a kite that waits the wind.

Or take

> Muhammad loved but God Almighty,
>   My mistress, mark you, was not born.

or

> Of gold be the mat and golden the pillows
>   But the arms of my love are the pillow for me.

or

> I'd love to die at the beck of her finger,
>   Find my tomb in the palm of her hand.

[1]See Appendix A, p. 186.

or

> Big breakers roll over the sea,
> > Far sprayed by this wind from the west.
> A riddle come answer for me!
> > What, I pray, is this love in the breast?
>
> My homestead's with lightning aflame;
> > Over yours there is thunder a-roll.
> Seven heavens in one mortal frame,
> > That's the meaning of love in the soul.

Incidents from common life, colloquial language, imaginative colouring that presents ordinary things in an unusual aspect, the expression of ideas associated in a state of excitement, the incorporation of the passions of men with beautiful and permanent forms of nature, these, thought Wordsworth, went together to make up good poetry—certainly they are found in the best Malay *pantun*.

[1] See Appendix A, p. 186.

A Trengganu Fishing Boat

[face p. 160

9: ARTS AND CRAFTS

IN THE quadrangular and beaked adzes of Malaya's late neolithic (2000–1500 B.C.) slept the talent of a race destined to carve the bas-reliefs of Bara-Budur and Prambanan. Static crouching figures with hands folded over knee or chest, crude stone sculpture from Java and Sumatra, have been ascribed to this Indonesian stone culture. To-day this primitive megalithic art survives among the Nagas of Assam, in Luzon and on the island of Nias; buffalo *motifs* in Celebes designs indicate its passage down to Oceania. In Malaya, if it is to be traced at all, it has lasted in the shape of a brooch (*dokoh*) which especially in Negri Sembilan continues to display its derivation from the buffalo-horns that adorn the roof-trees of Batak houses and are memorials of the feasts given by the Malay's neolithic ancestors to increase their prestige in this world and the next.

But through the Malay peninsula there passed a few centuries before Christ another people, perhaps the Yues (ancestors of the Annamites), perhaps Chams, who left behind bronze celts, three bell-shaped bronzes in Klang (Selangor) and fragments of two bronze drums, one at Klang and one in the Tembeling river. Their art was brought originally across Asia from Europe before 720 B.C. when the Scythians invading Russia also acquired it. One stream of migrants seems to have gone north and helped to destroy the Chou capital in 771 B.C.; another branched south to Yunnan and Indochina. Their art survives in many Indonesian motifs like the deer on textiles from the island of Sumba, and their craft of boat-building may be traced in boats on Singgora lake, at the island of Botel Tobago, in the Moluccas and Solomon islands and in the ancient Nordic bark of the dead that adorns cloths from Sumatra. The charateristics of their bronze-work were determined, after excavation at a place called Dong-so'n in Annam had revealed graves containing some twenty drums of the type found in Malaya as well as daggers and mirrors and coins that prove the latest contents of the graves to be relics of the Wang Mang period (9–22 A.D.). These characteristics are rectangular spirals, triangular spirals, rectangular spirals with moulded corners, double-S-shaped spirals and plaited bands, all of them types of ornamentation encountered in Yunnan, Laos, Sumatra, Java and the Sunda Islands, places where similar drums have been got. S-shaped spirals adorn one of the Dong-so'n bell-shaped bronzes from Klang, a bronze now in the British Museum, which also owns fragments of Dong-so'n bronzes from Yunnan. This style of art, which has been taken for a late branch of the Mycenaean, may be detected in ancient bronze vessels from China, in the painted designs on Batak houses, in carved bamboos of the Minangkabau, in some *batik* patterns and even in the fretted openwork of Java's shadow puppets. A resemblance has been surmised between a house on piles with bird-headed roof-tree depicted on a Dong-so'n drum from Ngoc-lu in Tonkin and the houses of the Kachens of Burma, the Ao-Nagas of Assam, the Torajas of Celebes, the Toba Bataks and the Minangkabau Malays. Houses on a drum from Bima are of Batak type. But the most startling evidence of influence in Malaysia from what, after the site of the graves, is generally termed Dong-so'n art, comes from the textiles of Lampong in Sumatra.

For the women weavers of Lampong are still adepts at dyeing ceremonial hangings for funerals and festivals with immemorial patterns that like some Dayak paintings represented a stylised bark for the dead with the tree of life for its mast and occasionally with men in feathered head-dress. Woven mats from Lampong still show this design. One of its notable features is that, as in Dayak basketry and some *batik* cloths, a bold pattern stands out against a background of spirals and meanders, recalling beyond dispute early bronzes from China. The decoration of the barks with angular spirals and plaited bands, here a hornbill, there a bifurcated stern, masts adorned with feathers, men in the feathered head-dress of the modern Dayak or

Naga, all these details are common to these Lampong cloths and to the bronze drums of Dong-so'n art, which included elements not only from Halstatt, Thrace and Caucasia but from the Nordic Bronze Age.

Dong-so'n drums depict shamans in feathered headdress, hornbills and deer. Deer frequently form a motif in a design on cloths from the islands of Sumba (in the Sunda group), a design that starting probably from Caucasia spread to Siberia and as early as the Han period (206 B.C.—200 A.D.) to China. In one Sumba specimen two large animals, apparently horses, face a bark for the dead. The more usual pattern is one of two horses facing a round-headed giant or, in Sumba, facing a tree sometimes surmounted by a sun and rays:—comparative study has discovered the sun in the round head of the giant and its rays in his hair, and it has traced the tree form in the single pedestal that takes the place of feet in the giant. The two horses have, perched on their backs, birds, especially the cock, a bird like them sacred to the sun, the slayer of serpents that appear so often in Sumba cloths.[1] By the nomads horses were killed for the use of a chief in the next world, and the conservatism of a people who had tamed the reindeer first led sometimes to such horses being disguised as deer. So there is nothing strange in the horses on Sumba cloths often being replaced by two deer[2] or by cocks that salute the sun. For the pattern of two animals facing a tree has been traced back in all its varieties to sun worship (of which perhaps Malaya has a relic in the cart-wheel design on the handles of coconut spoons carved in Kelantan, that is identical with a sun-ray design on Lapp spoons). The solar disks, the boats, the spirals, the deer, the processions of birds, that figure upon the Dong-so'n drums, have all been taken to suggest that their makers were sun-

[1] The pattern of a bird on the back of an animal occurs in Sumerian art of the 3rd and on a Syro-Hittite seal of the 2nd millenium B.C., on pottery of the 9th century B.C. from Sialk in Persia, at Harappa and on a Halstattian bronze.

[2] The huge stylized tails of most of these deer may, I hazarded once, be survivals of wings. Now Dr. R. von Heine-Geldern tells me that winged horses do occur on a Sumba cloth in a private collection in New York. But whence came this griffin? Probably Sumba patterns may be derived from more than one source.

worshippers. Some, however, consider the disks on the drums to be the pole-star of Babylonian cosmology. And stone disks with large central holes (like two unearthed at Kenaboi with two bronze socketted celts and resembling the Chinese *pi*) have been found in Kelantan as bracelets on skeletal remains. Yet as sun-worship is associated with a tree of life, it is perhaps significant that at Jelebu, not far from Kenaboi, the tree of life is still represented by a young plantain held erect by a maiden on the bier of the (Muslim) territorial chieftain or Dato' Mandulika. But if ever the tin-miners of Kenaboi introduced their weaving at some Jelebu village or on the Tembeling river, its patterns have long been extinguished by Hindu influences, although study of the patterns on Senoi dart-cases and blow-pipes might yield results, seeing that Senoi dialects were affected by these bronze-age visitors.

On sculpture as well as weaving the Dong-so'n civilization left its mark in the Malay world. In the Pasemah district of Sumatra there occur along with slab-graves (like those in the Batang Padang district of Perak) pieces of sculpture of a vigorous dynamic style quite unlike the static Indonesian type. Von Heine-Geldern compares them with plausibility to the tomb-stones of the Chinese general Huo K'iu-ping erected in Shensi province in 117 B.C. Two pieces represent men riding buffaloes, one represents a man fighting an elephant, one an elephant carrying a man with a Dong-so'n drum on his back. Unfortunately none of this sculpture has been found in Malaya.

As early as the 7th century B.C. China had monopolies for salt and iron, and the people of the Dong-so'n civilization were acquainted with the use of iron. The three bell-shaped Dong-so'n bronzes from Selangor (one is in the British and one in the Taiping Museum) were dug up at Klang along with three iron tools, common in Malaya, the so-called "ape's bones" (*tulang mawas*) that appear as weapons on Khmer bas-reliefs and survive in the modern *pkhéak* of

Cambodia. But whether people from China or Indo-China or India were responsible for the change in the Malay world from bronze tools and weapons to iron is still a matter for conjecture. The affinities of the rich variety of choppers of the *parang* and *golok*[1] type, the origin of the lance (*tombak*) and spear (*lembing*), the origin of a widely-spread dagger (*badik*), all these await study. Bronze knives of 1000 B.C. from An-yang and bronze knives from Ordos in Mongolia together with the heart-shaped guard of the Scythian sword are identical with the shape and guard of the Malay dagger known as the "pepper-crusher" (*tumbok lada*), the sole difference being that in the An-yang and Ordos knives blade and hilt are in one piece and the Malay dagger has a detachable hilt. But an example of the transition from the one-piece dagger to the dagger with a separate hilt lies to hand in the history of the creese, the only Malay weapon that has received adequate attention.

The creese (*keris*)—as Milton and Tennyson Englished it—is mentioned as early as the 9th century A.D. in an inscription of the Sailendra period. According to a Javanese tradition recorded by Raffles it reached Java from Malaya when the peninsula was subject to Majapahit in the 14th century. But the *provenance* and nomenclature of early specimens (*keris Majapahit*) point to Java as its country of origin, although its prototype is again to be traced to the Dong-so'n culture and may therefore have been first met by the Javanese in Malaya. This two-edged dagger is not an Indonesian weapon nor does it appear among Indian weapons on the bas-reliefs of Bara-Budur or other early Indo-Javanese monuments or in the oldest Kelantan version of the shadow-play of the Ramayana. So the creese can have neither an Indonesian nor an Indian origin. The type first appears in the 14th century on Chandi Panataran, where, however, it is closer to the Bugis *sundang* or short sword. And the oldest form of creese proper is the Majapahit iron creese, in which as in the Dong-so'n bronze daggers

---

[1]Mahmud, last Sultan of Malacca, sent a bejewelled Pahang machete or *golok* to the Raja of Pasai wiht a request for a solution of a Sufi conundrum.

blade and hilt are forged in one piece. The blades of these early creeses have curves but curves so slight and clumsy that they are reputed to have been fashioned by the smith's fingers. Hilts are of two types. The first type, like those on the Dong-so'n daggers, consists of a figure standing with hands on thighs, reminiscent of primitive ancestral figures from Nias and Luzon, and so, we may surmise, compact of Indonesian and Dong-so'n blends. The second type of Majapahit hilt is still of one piece with the blade, but it represents a figure squatting, elbows down and hands on knees, a figure still fashioned under Dong-so'n influence and in an Indonesian posture but borrowed from Hindu mythology.

For links between the squatting Indonesian posture and Hindu iconography von Heine-Geldern has pointed to the half-sitting, half-kneeling Raksasa or giant guardian of a monument at Singosari and to the famous terracotta Garuda of Belahan kneeling to support the Javanese ruler Erlangga in his incarnation as Vishnu. And as evidence of the date of the switch-over from a one-piece weapon to a creese with separate hilt of gold, ivory or wood, he quotes a passage from the Old-Javanese Ramayana, concluding that the change took place at the end of the 13th century or earlier. The blade, too, became wavy to represent Nagas, of whom in Hindu myth Garuda was the traditional slayer.

For creese hilts commonly represent Vishnu's bird the Garuda (wingless but sometimes beaked) or a Raksasa or very rarely Hanuman. In Heine-Geldern's view the Raksasa hilt stands for the demon cannibal Kalmasapada of a Jataka tale. Like that ogre, the Garuda also was a devourer of men, and Hanuman, though not an eater of men, yet like Kalmasapada in his Rahu form tried to eat the sun. All three of these mythical figures possessed supernatural strength, were invulnerable and could fly and darken the earth by their flight. The Garuda and Hanuman were of great stature, could assume different shapes and become invisible and they were skilled leeches. Like Hanuman,

ARTS AND CRAFTS 167

Kalmasapada was a mighty jumper. In short all three of the figures chosen to adorn a creese-hilt had magical qualities that their presentment might convey to the owner of the dagger.

Probably von Heine-Geldern is right in thinking the Raksasa hilt represents specifically the demon cannibal Kalmasapada of the Maha-Sutasoma Jataka, the tusked cannibal king of the Kedah Annals. This Buddhist tale had so wide a vogue that, as he points out, a scene from it has provided a *motif* for a sword-hilt from Laos and one of the *motifs* for a highly stylized hilt for Nias and Dayak swords, the Kalmasapada of Dayak hilts resembling 13th century Kala heads from East Java. "The Batak," too, "like the Burmese and Shan, use two varieties of it. The first shows the ogre Kalmasapada carrying King Sutasoma, whom he has ravished, on his shoulders, while the second version depicts the giant animal-headed ogre squatting behind the standing Sutasoma ready to devour him."

The Garuda on the oldest type of Javanese hilt, a type alien to Malaya, is a comic dwarf with staring eyes and beak-like nose. There is, however, another type found in different shapes in Java Madura Celebes and south Sumatra, that on a human body has the bird face of the Garuda. One wonders if its inventors with the Indonesian passion for syncretism had in mind the bird-men servitors of death on the Dong-so'n drums and the Lampong cloths? Lampong, Patani and Kelantan examples of this second type of hilt have a long beak that in Malaya has won it the name of the king-fisher (*pekaka*) hilt, *pekaka* being a corruption of Chikakak, the name of a Javanese puppet figure. This king-fisher creese from the north of Malaya has a large curved cross-piece of Javanese pattern for its sheath, and its makers bore the Javanese name (*pandai*) for smith, so that it must be a relic of Majapahit domination in the 14th century. The third type of creese-hilt, and in Malaya the commonest, is one the Bugis of Celebes carried all over the Malay world. The bowed head and folded arms of this compact stylized hilt have won it the nickname of "the fevered Javanese" (*Jawa demam*), although in fact the head is still that of a bird. Practically all creese-hilts are variations of the Raksasa and Garuda types, even the latest stylized "pistol-butt" hilt still often retaining traces of a beaked head, though Islam has abolished definite symbols of Hindu Garuda and Raksasa.

Hindu influence on the blades of other weapons and knives has still to be traced. But it is noteworthy that a heavy Indian falchion was familiar to Malays from the 9th or 10th century (when a miniature of it was buried under a Kedah sanctuary) and it even figures centuries later on Javanese bas-reliefs, but it never came to be a Malay weapon. Again, the Malays knew *churika*, the Prakrit word for "knife", but apart from an erroneous Batak ascription of it to a *parang* and an erroneous Perak ascription of it to a state sword, the name is applied (1) to a heavy spatulate dagger of the Raksasas of Prambanan and Singosari, a dagger that is one of the Minangkabau regalia and was used for tantric sacrifices, and also (2) to a heavy chopper of the type employed to-day by Tamils for ritual slaughter. Falchions, and knives bearing the name *churika* were Indian and never adopted in the Malay world.

For, except in the sphere of sculpture and of gold and silver and brass work, Hindu influence did less for arts and crafts in the Malay world than was done by the older cultures from China and Indo-China. It spread less widely. It failed to supplant the Malay types of sea-going craft. It failed to quash the older designs on Dayak, Batak, Sumba and Lampong textiles and it made no headway against the *batik* of Java and Bali.

Small Buddhist stupas and Hindu temples dating from the 4th to the 10th century have been unearthed in Kedah, but all are the work of Indian colonists. A Hinayana Buddha of Amaravati style from Kedah, two of pure Gupta style from Perak, two eight-armed Avalokitesvaras of Pala type with tantric emblems from Kinta and Bidor are all of them either purely Indian bronzes or close imitations of Indian prototypes. From Bangka, however, there comes a four-armed stone figure with cylindrical head-dress that combines Indian characteristics with a Malay cast of features and appears to show how Pallavan art became in the 7th century Sri-Vijayan or Indo-Malayan. From such beginnings sprang the sculpture of Sumatra and the great sculpture of Java. But south of Jaiya, stone sculpture passed by the sparsely inhabited Malay peninsula, which has no carving to show except Malacca's stone Makara (that may have been brought from Sumatra), creese-hilts and the wood-carving on a few Minangkabau houses in Negri Sembilan.

It has been remarked that Indian influence on the textiles of Malaysia was not widely spread. But the nearness of Malaya to India and its constant trade with India made Indian cloths and Indian patterns the only wear at courts and extinguished any earlier patterns. The word for silk is borrowed from the Sanskrit, and India introduced silken fabrics into the Malaysian cotton area, at first for rajas only. To this day, silk-weaving is practised over a limited area, being confined to coastal states, courts and the larger towns. Java and Bali produce silk *batik*, and Celebes, Borneo and Sumatra weave other silks. In the Malay peninsula, Patani Kelantan and Trengganu (covering the region of ancient Sri Vijaya) have all been noted for their silk fabrics, and silk-weavers pursue their craft at a few other scattered places where some Sumatran expert has immigrated. The obsolescent "lime" pattern (*kain limau*) of Trengganu Kelantan and Pahang silks, a rich mottled "snake's head" blend of dark reds and greens, reminds one of Indian designs, though its tie-and-dye process (perhaps of Dong-so'n origin) differs from the Indian as "it is the warp threads before weaving that are tied and not the woven cloth". Trengganu also produced cloths where in Indian fashion a pattern of gold thread is inter-woven with the silk, sometimes with plain silk, sometimes with silk chequered with thin lines in white or blue, sometimes (*kain tenggarun*) with silk of the mottled "lime" pattern. This cloth of gold has been woven at other places too in Malaya, but none of the peninsular looms could vie with those of Batu Bara and Palembang in Sumatra. Patani, Pahang and Selangor produce cloths (*kain telepok*) gilded by a technique practised also in the Punjab. Cotton with a small pattern on a dark green or dark blue ground is polished (with cowry shells), stamped with carved wooden blocks that have been smeared with gum, and then covered with gold leaf that adheres to the gummy pattern. Yet another process, similar to one in the Punjab, is to impress a pattern on silk by means of small stamps containing only a flower or the section of a border. A good deal of the pattern is produced by stitching the cloth firmly together in puckers, and larger spaces which are not to take the dye are tied tightly in pieces of the skin of the leaf-stalk of the banana. The tied cloth is immersed in the dye for the ground colour. It is then allowed to dry, and the tying and stitching are undone. The fabric is next stretched on a frame to have patterns in various coloured dyes brushed, some in free-hand on the white spaces left and some on the coloured ground.

Chinese chronicles of the 10th century tell us how kings of Sumatra with Indian titles wore "flowered silk adorned with pearls" and used "canopies of feathers and embroidered curtains". They also tell us how an Emperor of China at the beginning of the 15th century sent kings of Malacca "velvets, silks and gauzes embroidered with gold", "suits of clothes embroidered with dragons and one suit with kilins". Antique belts of scarlet cloth and silk trousers were beaded and had disks of tinfoil inlet, as they are inlet in Lampong and Dayak cloths still: these disks have been found in Khotan and are common in Indian and Chinese embroidery. Many influences must have been at work to produce the modern styles of Malay embroidery. The Perak court is especially famous for its embroidered mats and pillows. Two styles have been in vogue, flat surface embroidery and embroidery in raised relief. Foliated patterns are usual.

The earliest *repoussé* work found in Malaya is on lion-head (*simha-mukha*) clasps to two gold bracelets dug up at Fort Canning Singapore and on a lion-head buckle to a belt of woven gold wire fished out of the Batu Lintang river in Kedah only to be lost during the Japanese occupation. "Gold belts similarly ornamented are depicted on stone images in India from 9th century A.D." Dr. Quaritch-Wales is of opinion that the Kedah belt was probably made in the 13th century and that, as its lion-head has degenerated into a mere ornamental *motif* of foliage, it must be later than the Singapore bracelets. He compares it with a belt on the stone image of a Bhairava, perhaps King Adityavarman of Minangkabau, at Sungai Langsat, Sumatra. An engraven ring and a gemmed ring were found with the Singapore bracelets. Inlay of gold ornaments with semi-precious stones is seen, for example, in the Perak royal armlets. This art of inlay with stones or enamel was common in Mongolia, but it may have been taught to Javanese and Malays by Indian craftsmen.

In *repoussé* silverwork there are two predominant styles in Malaya, a northern and a southern, both pre-Islamic and indebted to India for their designs. Everywhere waist-buckles of silver gold and niello are ornamented with the large Buddhist lotus blossom. Some caskets have deep gadroons forming lotus petals like those at the base of Buddhist idols. In Perak open lotus-blooms like tiny roses abound on watch-shaped caskets and adorn decorative bands on large lidded bowls. A popular pattern is the so-called pine-apple pattern or side view of the lotus that occurs also on Bara-Budur (and has spread as far as Samarkand). The Hellenistic interlacing of volutes and some floral borders appear to be derived from the art of the Palas, which would have influenced northern Malaya, when it was part of Sri Vijaya. In the Riau-Johor water-vessels foliate and floral meanders, bands and pendants are usual, as in Pallava and other Indian carving. The more expert the Malay smith, the more flowers and foliage tend, though not excessively, towards the naturalistic, peony and chrysanthemum then being favourite motifs, as for example, in the Perak royal betel-box and Tengku Kamariah's 18th century betel-set in the Johor collection. One pattern called after the fern-shoot occurs also in Dayak ornament, and the full genealogy of the decoration on Malay silverwork has yet to be worked out. The Perak and Riau-Johor styles are differentiated not only by the prevalence of the lotus *motif* in the former and of foliate and floral meanders in the latter, but by two typical standard shapes. In Perak the largest water-vessel is lidded, spheroidal and surmounted by a small handle like the seed pod of the lotus with tiny jingling pendants. In Riau-Johor the largest water-vessel is an open bellied pot with a squat neck and lipped edges turning outwards. But apart from these vessels, different styles are confused and coexist in the same locality. The Malays have borrowed both shapes of early European watches, round and octagonal, for tobacco-boxes. There are also two types of lime boxes in the betel-sets. One is squat and of capstan shape and decorated with *repoussé* work, the other is round and often decorated with a gold filigree *plaque* on top of its oval lid.

For as common as *repoussé* is a kind of filigree that decorates neck pendants (*agok*), brooches (*dokoh*), the peacock-crowned cheese-scoup finger-guard, the obsolete big round earring, the base of gold and silver creese-sheaths, the ring-mounting of creese and spear, the *plaques* on betel caskets and on large round silver boxes. It reminds one of south Indian filigree and may have been taken by Tamils direct to Sumatra. For Raffles has recorded that "the Javans do not as a rule work gold into those beautiful filigree patterns common among Malays of Sumatra". A highly stylized foliate pattern is fashioned of raised gold (or silver) wire, fine as cotton and twisted like cotton in strands, and this pattern is, as it were pinned down by tiny pin-heads or fish-eggs, as the Malays call them, which are sometimes enlarged and wrought in the shape of very tiny conventional flowers. Filigree is sometimes jewelled. It used to be made a decade or so ago in Kuala Pilah and is probably still a living craft in Negri Sembilan.

Malay Silver-work and a Gold Waist-buckle

[face p. 172

ARTS AND CRAFTS 173

A few betel-scissors exist with silver or gold wire inset in an iron ground and, if of Malay craftsmanship closely copy south Indian patterns. A favourite pattern was that of a horse with a Tamil name (*kuda sembrani* = *cemburani*, "bay"). Creeses sometimes had Arabic texts and charms inlaid in gold or silver. Waist-buckles are found of oxydised copper with a gold inlay.

In Negri Sembilan tobacco and lime caskets and, commonest of all, waist-buckles are made of a kind of niello (*jadam*) a silver pattern obtained by the *repoussé* method being filled with a blue-black sulphide. The Buddhist lotus pattern is universal on these niello buckles and caskets. There are also brass waist-buckles with cutch inlay and lotus decoration.

The most ornate of all workmanship in silver is a niello (*chutam*) from Ligor in Siamese Malaya, specimens of which were common in Perak and Kedah. One account says it was made by Malays captured in the wars between Kedah and Siam. Another account says that it flourished in Ligor from the 12th or 13th century down to the middle of the 18th. Clearly, if Malay, the ware antedates Islam. But the contour of its bowls is different from the half coconut-shell contour of the ordinary Malay bowl. Spouted water-kettles with pyramidal lids and swinging handles are common; many are of Chinese shape. The lotus form predominates in the shapes of large water-bottle stands and pedestal dishes but it is not found in the decoration, of which there are two kinds: the older a chaste foliation in which were introduced snakes, squirrels, deer and figures from the Ramayana, the more modern a profuse and delicate stylized foliation that left little of the black background visible. It is still made at an art school in Bangkok.

Bronze articles have died out before imported wares. But formerly the best Malay cannon were cast in bronze, as also were some censers trays and bowls. A mixture of tin with a little copper and antimony is used in Trengganu for the manufacture of trade betel-trays and boxes. But the bulk of Malay household utensils are of brass. All bronze, copper and brass work has a Sanskrit name to its metal, though *gangsa*, the word for bronze, is now hardly understood, and *tembaga* "brass" is applied to all the alloys, with the attribute "red" to distinguish copper. Articles are cast by the *cire perdue* process, and when the mould has cooled, the outer shell is broken and the rough metal article is smoothed on a lathe. Heavy bowls and lamps are copies of Indian ware. Trays and large lidded boxes are thin and decorated with realistic representations of butterflies, deer, flowers and birds, output for the most part from Palembang. There are glass stands and betel-trays decorated with petty fretted patterns. All but the heavy articles are immeasurably below the Dong-so'n standard.

Pottery of the neolithic inhabitants of Malaya has been found in large quantities in caves. "It is hardly too much to say that no two vessels are alike. Their chief interest lies in their diversity of form ... ornamentation was relatively unambitious; cordmarking is the most usual form of ornament. Simple incised patterns are found. The ware is generally dark in colour with sand and charcoal tempering and often a polished surface produced by burnishing with the application of soot." Study of this pottery has not yet proceeded far. At Srokam in Kedah Dr. Quaritch Wales discovered along with Sung (A.D. 960–127) or early Yuan (1260–1368) celadon a few potsherds with stamped lotus designs. Pottery with somewhat similar lotus designs has been found at Kota Tinggi on the Johor river, everywhere along with Ming (1368–1644) porcelain. Pottery with a stamped herring-bone design has been dug up both at Kota Tinggi and Johor Lama. Both kinds bear a close resemblance to pottery excavated at Han period kilns in Annam, and even if the ware is too fragile to have been imported and differs from Han ware in its chemical content, it must be assumed to be of Chinese origin.

Local variations persist in Malay pottery to-day. The stamped herring-bone pattern common at both Johor sites is characteristic of modern pottery from Perlis. In Perak pottery water-vessels modelled on the shape of a gourd are nearer in form to bronze-age flasks from a Sumatran urn-grave than to any Javanese forms illustrated in Dr. Stutterheim's "Pictorial History". From Pahang, especially from Kuala Tembeling, come pieces bearing stamps of superior decorative quality, sometimes spouted and having often as the *motif* of their form the short arc rather than the rounded almost circular curve. Common in Malacca were water-jars coloured a dull brownish black and stamped deep to look like florid wood carvings. Some of these types may be due to foreign influences in modern times. For the Malay potter seems long ago to have lost the invention and artistry of his neolithic ancestors.

"Fine mats" are cited among exports from Johor by Chinese chroniclers three hundred years ago. There are three chief methods of adornment—in mats, open-work and the interweaving of strips dyed red, black and yellow to produce diaper patterns; in mats and especially in baskets, the plaiting of raised fancy twists by a method practised in Malacca and termed the "mad plait". Dish covers are sometimes made of this mad plait, or they are made of strips of the white inner sheath of bamboo dyed red or black and cut into open-work patterns that are stuck over a conical *mengkuang* lining shaped like Chinese hats.

10: THE FUTURE

For many reasons the lessons of history are neglected in the modern world. Darwin turned the eyes of the sanguine away from the past to the future, and those who in spite of war and atrocities still believe in progress towards some mundane paradise prefer the doubtful promise of science to the record of man's puerilities, errors and crimes. Yet physical science with its atomic bomb may bring evil as well as good to mankind, nor may political theory, even when it has been tried out with success in Europe, suit the needs of Asia, though it come in the plausible guise of communism or democracy. The only way to see beyond one's nose for the promotion of a race's welfare is to review the effect of past practice and endeavour and to study the social, political, economic and spiritual history of the race that is to be the subject of experiment.

Recent Malay social advance it is easy to summarise. In the earliest days of protection, the British insisted on the abolition of slavery, an immemorial blot on Malay civilisation. It is possible that the British engaged in its abolition exaggerated the universality of gross ill-treatment, but the system of bondage common among Indo-Chinese races was less elastic than that among the Arabs, and resulted in a helot class whose members seldom or never escaped thraldom or rose to place and office. Not only did the British abolish slavery in Malaya, but they replaced the exactions of chiefs by a uniform system of taxation, and abrogated such mediaeval penalties as lopping off the hands of thieves and creesing those guilty of what tribal custom termed incest. The freeman was no longer debarred by fear of ancient sumptuary laws from extending his fields, building a decent house and buying his wife and daughters jewellery. By education and example the British also encouraged the emancipation of Malay women, who have now advanced so far that, instead of retreating behind their menfolk, they are ready, in spite of being Muslims, to enter the political arena.

Altered economic conditions have for some years promoted monogamy even among rajas and chiefs, with whom polygamy was formerly universal, a change making not only for the happiness of women but for the welfare of children. So far, however, as divorce is concerned, the need of the agriculturist for a family persists and encourages the repudiation of childless wives. At the same time the spread of education among girls is calculated to create intellectual ties between the sexes that will not be broken merely by barrenness. Only in one respect is there any likelihood that modern conditions may be adverse to women; an enhanced regard for Muslim law being liable to damage their customary rights to property on death or divorce. However, the intellectual alertness of both sexes to their rights and prospects depends on good health, and the town Malay and to a lesser extent the Malay of the countryside have benefitted by the introduction of preventive and curative medicine, being no longer without remedies for complaints like yaws or without measures against plague, small-pox and malarial infection. Improved health should see greater physical and mental effort in the Malay race. Education has already rid the Malay of ghostly terrors, and taking the professions, trade and agriculture to be its province has provided his race with fresh equipment for the battle of life. Having to learn to read the Kuran in Arabic, a language he does not understand, is a strain on the Malay child that is not undergone by the other races of Malaya. But the educational system has produced Malays who have taken honours at Cambridge and have been called to the bar and qualified as doctors and engineers. Continued social progress will depend on the extension of all types of education suited to local needs, and that extension will depend on satisfactory political and economic conditions.

As for those political conditions, Malaya provides a signal example of how men of the same race may differ according to their geographical circumstances and systems of government. The people of Minangkabau, whether in Sumatra or in Negri Sembilan, having lived inland away from foreign contacts for centuries have preserved a primitive democracy and treated royalty as a magical excrescence on their ancient tribal constitution. The Malays of port kingdoms on the contrary were led by promise of trade to accept the leadership of rulers and chiefs with a strain of Indian blood in their veins, and so with the tradition and practice of commerce behind them. But whether under the matrilineal democracy of Negri Sembilan or the patriarchal autocracy of other States, the Malay always suffered from failure to respect the will of the majority. In Negri Sembilan complete unanimity was necessary for the election of chiefs, and as unanimity is seldom or never attainable, civil strife or at the best procrastination was universal until the British gave decision to the majority vote of a State Council. In patriarchal States, the council of chiefs, that everywhere survived and accompanied the institution of kingship, again found its ancient ideal of unanimity unattainable and so would frequently bow to the despotism of a Sultan who was generally swayed by his strongest adviser. In 1446 a youthful Sultan of Malacca was murdered to make way for one with the blood of a prominent Tamil merchant in his veins. At the beginning of the 19th century five claimants disputed the throne of Negri Sembilan. From 1857 to 1863 two brothers fought for the throne of Pahang. In the '60s there was civil war in Selangor owing to the Sultan's inability to govern unruly chiefs. In the '70s Perak was the scene of Chinese faction fights which a disputed succession to the throne made it harder to suppress. Too often a Malay ruler had little except fear of his divine majesty to enforce his will, and relatives often had little respect for that obsolescent divinity and fought him for the throne. Moreover dense forests cut up the little Malay kingdoms into districts where local chiefs did what was right in their own eyes. These difficulties were surmounted under British protection. Great Britain kept the peace and introduced the reign of law. Roads and railways consolidated each State. Chiefs learnt in State Councils the advantages of majority rule. But there was another side to this political picture. Except in States like Kedah and Johor, which before they came under British protection had educated chiefs, the tendency was for Malays to sink into complete dependence upon British advice and to lose initiative. One result of the Japanese war was an awakening of a Malay political sense which must be wholly good for the race, though it is bound to strengthen prejudice against any continued large immigration of foreigners, especially Chinese, for work on tin mines and rubber estates. When they entered the Malay States, the British persuaded the Malays for the first time in their history to admit without demur infidels, British, Chinese and Indian, to their State Councils and to open the ranks of the subordinate civil service to a flood of alien Asiatics. But since those early days tin and rubber have attracted swarms of Indians to Malaya and so many Chinese that they equal in number the Malays themselves. The British initiated the policy of admitting permanent settlers to citizenship, and this may possibly be countered by a Malay endeavour to limit immigration to Javanese and Sumatrans, men of their own blood and religion. Statesmanlike though many Malays are, independence faces no easy future. The mixed population of Malaya will make it exceedingly difficult. Political elections are as yet on trial. Chinese talent for politics even in China has yet to be proved, and, unless they were locally born and educated, the Chinese displayed no interest in Malayan politics; but the appearance of Malay nationalism has awakened them from their former apathy. It cannot be too often insisted that no political system can fuse races differing in colour, religion, civilisations and ideals, as Malays, Chinese and Indians differ. For such a society theory is inapplicable, and practice must be the touch-stone:—

> For forms of government let fools contest;
> Whate'er is best administer'd is best.

More important than experiments in ideal government is the improvement of economic conditions in Malaya. At the outset it must be premised that European and Malay ideas of comfort and happiness differ widely, nor is it easy for the European well-wisher to grasp all the profits of the Malay small-holder. It sounds and is scandalous that the net earnings of a Malay fisherman before the war was between £12 and £16 a year. Yet fishing is not his only source of livelihood, and the value of the fish his family consumes has to be added. Even under existing conditions his independent open-air life is infinitely preferable to that of a London clerk on £8 a week. Not long ago I heard a discussion as to the possibility of recruiting a married Malay for work in England on £600 a year. "With his family," said a Malay present, "he will be far better off in his own village on his pension of £100 a year." In Malaya there are no insurance schemes, but the Malays enjoy free medical attention and free education. Taxation is negligible. The price of land is small. The cost of building a house has been insignificant. Clothes are for ornament rather than for health. Most of a peasant's food comes from his own holding. If his rice-harvest fails, he no longer starves or subsists on tapioca; imported rice is conveyed to him by train and lorry. Peace and science have brought him profits from crops like copra. The world's demand for rubber has made many Malays rich beyond their dreams. In spite of all this, the vast majority of Malays, like most other peoples of Asia, live on the brink of indigence, and the most urgent of all needs is to raise the standard of living by improving methods of agriculture and fishing, modernizing the system of marketing and inculcating the thrift that ensures expenditure on useful as opposed to outmoded ends, which modern conditions have made extravagant. These measures are the more urgent, because some day Malaya's tin will be worked out, and natural rubber may suffer from competition with synthetic. It is a mistake to regard Malaya as a country with a rich tropical soil. Most of it has poor soil fit only to grow a hardy crop like rubber. Nor if rubber failed would it be easy to find any other crop in sufficient demand to take its place.

In the realm of art and literature the Malay is under

severe handicaps. It is centuries since art flourished in any Muhammadan country and the Muslim construction of the Second Commandment still narrows its field to abstract and geometrical forms. If art ever flowers again in the Malay world, the seed is likely to come from Java where once it flourished. As for Malay literature, hitherto it has been a literature of translation. The Malay is still a child of nature in a sophisticated world that awaits his exploration. If any Malay should develop an original literary bent, it is more likely that the impulse will come from densely populated Java or even from Sumatra rather than from the two and a half million Malays of the peninsula, though it is not always the probable that happens.

APPENDICES

A. MALAY TEXT OF PASSAGES CITED IN THE CHAPTERS

Page 27
Hunuskan pedang, bakarkan sarong,
Ithbatkan Allah, nafikan patong.

Page 32
Bismi 'llahi 'r-Rahmani 'r-Rahimi!
Bakar bakar pasir tanah!
Aku bakar mata hati jantong (si-anu) itu.
Bakar-ku panah Sang Rajuna.
Aku bakarkan di-gunong, gunong runtoh;
Aku bakarkan di-batu, batu belah;
Aku bakarkan di-mata hati jantong hawa nafsu (si-anu),
Kena hanchor luloh panas segala tuboh-nya,
Gila berahi ka-pada aku,
Tidak boleh senang diam,
Saperti pasir ini terbakar.
Benchi-lah (si-anu) ka-pada ibu bapa,
Ka-pada saudara sahabat handai-nya;
Jika dia tidor, menjaga;
Jika dia jaga, bangun berjalan
Datang ka-pada aku
Menyerahkan diri-nya,
Hilang 'akal, hilang malu,
Berkat (si-anu) kena bisa panah Sang Rajuna,
Berkat do'a, La ilaha illa 'llah, Muhammadun Rasūlu 'llah.

Page 36
Bukan aku melepaskan bala pustaka,
Sang Kaki Batara Guru melepaskan bala pustaka!
Bukan aku melepaskan bala pustaka,
Dēwa keyangan melepaskan bala pustaka!
Bukan aku melepaskan bala pustaka,
Dēwa ketujoh melepaskan bala pustaka;
Bukan aku melepaskan bala pustaka,
Dēwa kesakti melepaskan bala pustaka;
Hai anak Bhatara Kala, chichit bhuta Singa Gana,
Turun lepaskan bala pustaka!
Turun lepaskan perbuatan manusia!
Lepaskan bala pustaka, chelaka malang!
Lepaskan 'pada rumah tangga dan segala anak Adam!

Parang Bisnu di-muka aku!
Hai jin, si-Raja Jin,
Jin nan megang tanah ayer,
Jin nan memangku bumi,
Pulang engkau ka-tempat engkau
Di-pusat tasēk tebing runtoh!
Jangan engkau masok tapak guru aku!
Jikalau engkau masok tapak guru aku,
Aku sumpah engkau dengan perkataan Nabi Allah Sulaiman,
Aku sumpah engkau dengan perkataan, La ilaha illa'llah,
   Muhammadun Rasūlu'llah.

PAGES 40–1
Bismi 'llahi 'r-Rahmani 'r-Rahimi!
Aku rebus (pasir) ini, aku uap (pasir) ini
   dengan panah kudrat Allah.
Aku melakukan kehendak Allah;
Aku mengambil ini dengan ma'rifat Allah.
Aku panahkan di-gunong, gunong rebah;
Aku panahkan di-batu, batu belah.

PAGE 41
Aku-lah yang sa-benar-benar Muhammad;
Bukan aku yang berkata;
Muhammad yang sa-benar-benar,
Muhammad yang berkata.
Dahulu ruh, kemudian jasad.
Petang ini ibu-ku;
Binasa malam ini, binasa-lah aku;
Jika ta' binasa malam ini,
Putus-lah sakalian, ta' binasa aku.
Ujud-mu ujud aku,
Ujud aku sa-ujud dengan-mu.
Ghaib-lah aku di-dalam kandang
La ilaha illa' llah,
Kandang ibu-ku nur Muhammad
Hingga sampai siang esok.

ib.

Puchik-ku tersandar di-tiang arash;
Allah mengulur, Muhammad menyambut.

PAGE 61
Orang semenda bertempat semenda.
Jikalau cherdēk, teman berunding;
Jikalau bodoh, di-suroh di-arah.
Tinggi, banir tempat berlindong;

Rimbun dahan tempat bernaung;
Orang semenda pergi karna suroh,
Berhenti karna tegah.
Jikalau ma'alim, hendakkan do'a-nya;
Jikalau kaya, hendakkan ĕmas;
Jikalau patah, penghalau ayam;
Jikalau buta, penghembus lesong.
Jikalau pekak, pembakar bedil.
Masok kandang kerbau, menguak;
Masok kandang kambing, membēbēk;
Bagai-mana 'adat tempat semenda, di-pakai.
Orang semenda dengan orang tempat semenda
Bagai mentimun dengan durian,
Menggolēk pun luka, kena golēk pun luka.

Page 84
Hati gajah sama di-lapah,
Hati kuman sama di-chichah;
Chichir sama rugi,
Mendapat sama laba.

Page 87
Raja sa-keadilan;
Penghulu sa-undang;
Tali pengikat dari-pada lembaga;
Keris penyalang dari-pada undang;
Pedang memanchong dari-pada keadilan,
Tikam, ta' bertanya,
Panchong, ta' berkhabar.

Page 89
Bulat ayēr karna pematong;
Bulat manusia karna muafakat.

Page 93
'adat bertanda, hukum bersaksi;
'adat yang tiba ka-gelap menjala ...
Bersurih ba'(gai) si-pasin,
Berlondar ba' lengkitang,
Berbau ba' machang;
Ka-hulu, ta' tentu gaung-nya,
Ka-hilir, ta' tentu kuala ...
Mana anjing menyalak, di-situ biawak memanjat.

Page 96
Sawah yang berjinjang,
Pinang yang gayu,
Nyior yang saka,
Lembaga yang punya.

Sah batal ka-pada kadim;
Kata berchari ka-pada waris-nya;
Tinggal waris, menongkat;
Tinggal sa-kadim, melintang;
Tinggal harta bertuan, ta' jadi;
Tinggal tua, batal.

Page 154
Turuni-lah londaran naga;
'Nak tahu pulau yang menumpu,
Tanyakan pada denak;
'Nak tahu padang yang luas,
Tanyakan pada bilalang;
'Nak tahu pulau yang panjang,
Tanyakan pada barau-barau.

ib.
Tengah malam sudah terlampau,
Dinihari belum lagi tampak;
Budak-budak dua kali jaga,
Orang muda pulang bertandang;
Orang tua berkalēh tidor;
Embun jantan rintēk-rintēk;
Bunyi kuang jauh ka-tengah,
Sering-lanting riang di-rimba;
Terdenguh lembu di-padang,
Sambut menguak kerbau di-kandang;
Bertepok mandong, merak mengigal;
Fajr sadi 'menyingsing naik;
Kichak-kichau bunyi murai;
Taptibau melambong tinggi;
Menguku balam di-ujong bendul,
Terdengut puyoh panjang bunyi;
Puntong sa-jengkal tinggal sa-jari.
Itu-lah 'alamat hari 'nak siang.

Pages 154-5
(Angin) nyaru-nyarang nyiru tembaga,
Kedua si-hampar rebah,
Ketiga lambing bertelinga,
Keempat Israfil sangka-kala;
Angin yang bergambar orang,
Yang menchabut chekor di-laman
Dan menchabut mali-mali di-lumpor
Dan merebah kerbau di-padang
Dan menyapu nyior dara di-laman balai.
Angin berkerusi karang tembaga;
Belanak main di-tinjau kurong,
Yu bermain di-pintu kurong.

ib.
Suara-nya berlagu-lagu;
Kera di-dahan jatoh menengar;
Burong yang terbang berhenti-henti;
Ayēr yang hilir berbalēk mudēk.

Page 156
Satukan hangat dan dingin,
Tinggalkan loba dan ingin,
Hanchor hendak saperti lilin,
Mangka-nya dapat kerja-mu lichin.

Pages 159–60
Asal kapas menjadi benang,
   Asal benang menjadi kain.
Yang lepas jangan di-kenang,
   Sudah menjadi orang lain.

Layang-layang kertas putēh,
   Budak-budak main di-tēmbok.
Kasēh sayang dengan chē' Utēh
   Laksana perahu membuang ombak.

Bukan mudah bercherai kasēh,
   Sa-bagai wau menanti angin.

Nabi Muhammad berchintakan Allah.
   Di-mana-lah tuan masa itu?

Tikar emas, bantal suasa,
   Mana sama bantal di-lengan?

Hendak mati di-ujong kuku;
   Hendak berkubur di-tapak tangan.

Angin barat gelombang barat,
   Barat memechah dari sa-berang.
Kalau adēk tahu 'ibarat,
   Apa maana kasēh sayang?

Berdentong guroh di-Papan,
   Kilat-nya sampai ka-Selayang.
Tujoh shurga di-dalam badan,
   Itu-lah maana kasēh sayang.

B. RELATIONSHIPS IN NEGRI SEMBILAN

RELATIONSHIP by Minangkabau custom is reckoned only on the distaff side, and in the Minangkabau colonies of the Negri Sembilan the same system obtains. A mother is *emak, ibu* or *indok*[1]; her child, *anak*; a grand-child, *chuchu*[2]; a great-grand-child, *chichit*; a great-great-grand-child, *piut*; and the two generations below are termed *oneng-oneng* and *antah-antah*. All women in the family of a mother's generation have the *pangkat* or standing of mother to her child. A grandmother is *wan*[3] (or in the language of strangers, *dato'*). All women in the family of a grandmother's generation have the *pangkat* of *wan* to her grandchild. A great-grandmother[4] is *ninēk*; a great-great-grandmother,[5] *onyang* or *moyang*. All women of those respective generations have the *pangkat* of that generation to their descendants. Hence often confusion. At the hearing of a claim to land three or four women will declare they have the same mother or grandmother or great-grandmother, when several of them mean really to say "aunt" or "grand-aunt" or "great-grand-aunt". Only after enquiry will they condescend to definite terms of relationship. There are such terms. A maternal aunt[6] is *emak sanak ibu* or *indok sanak ibu*; a maternal grand-aunt, *wan sanak ibu*; great-grand-aunt, *ninēk sanak ibu*. Conversely, a nephew or niece on the mother's side is *sanak ibu*; grand-nephew or grand-niece, *sanak dato'*[7]; great-grand-nephew or niece, *sanak ninēk*[8]; great-great-grand-nephew or niece, *sanak moyang*.[9] As the relationship becomes remote, generally it becomes vague in the absence of all records except oral tradition; and descendants describe themselves merely as *sa-ninēk, sa-moyang, sanak jauh*[10] or *sa-waris*, that

[1] *Indok* outside Negri Sembilan is used only of the "dam" of animals; in N.S. it is used even of "the centre of a house", *indok rumah*.

[2] Minangkabau distinguishes *chuchu kandong* lit. "grand-child of the womb" from *chuchu*, "grand-child" or "grand-nephew" (or niece). N.S. uses the latter for "grand-child" and *sanak dato* for "grand-nephew" (or niece).

[3] Min. *tuo* (=*tua*), *gaik, uchi*—the word *gaik* survives in N.S. in the phrase *tua gaik* = very old. Min. uses *tuo kandong, gaik kandong* to distinguish a "grandmother" from "grand-aunts", but N.S. has lost this useful distinction, and calls all *wan*.

[4] Min. *ninēk, ninēk moyang, andung*.

[5] *Ninēk moyang, poyang*, Min.

[6] *Mandēh*, Min.

[7] *Badansanak tuo*, b. *gaik*, Min.

[8] *Badansanak ninēk*.

[9] *Badansanak moyang*; the next generation is *badansanak poyang*.

[10] *Badansanak jauh:* all descended from the same ancestress are *saudara, sa-parinduan*.

is, as co-inheritors from the same female ancestress. The nearer relationships are very exact. The first-born in a Malay family is *Sulong, Ulong* or *Long*; the second, *Ngah*[1]; the third, *Alang* or *'Lang*; the fourth, *Andak*; the fifth, *Utēh*; the sixth, *Hitam*; the seventh, *Achik*; and the youngest *Bongsu* in other countries of the peninsula, but in the Negri Sembilan as in Minangkabau *Anchu* as well. These names are given to girls as well as to boys. With *'pa* set before them in the case of men and *mak* in the case of women, they serve to describe the exact status of a child's uncles and aunts. *'Pa Ngah* signifies for a child his second eldest uncle; *Mak Anchu*, his youngest aunt. These nicknames, fixed as regards the first four and last two, but uncertain sometimes in order as regards the intermediate, are given alike to maternal and to paternal aunts and uncles. A paternal aunt younger than one's father and a maternal aunt younger than one's mother are both called *"indok kechil*[2]; a maternal uncle younger than one's mother or a paternal uncle younger than one's father are alike *bapa kechil*.

Brothers and sisters are, as everywhere in the peninsula, *adēk-beradēk, saudara*; also, a description peculiar to N. Sembilan, *kadim*; if children of the same father and mother they are *saudara sa-indok sa-bapa* or *sa-kadim*; if uterine, *sanak* or *saudara sa-indok or sa-kadim*[3]; if of the same father only, *saudara sa-baka* or *sa-kadim*. An elder brother is *abang*, elder sister, *kakak*; eldest sister, *kakak tua*[4] or *'kak tua*; and younger brother or sister, *adēk*. Cousinship is reckoned like other degrees through mothers, that is on the distaff side. A cousin is *sanak ibu*; a female cousin, if older than oneself, *kakak sanak ibu*; a cousin younger than oneself, *adēk sanak ibu*.[5]

The term *sanak* corresponds to the Minangkabau term *dansanak dusanak* and describes a blood relation on the distaff side: children of a man by different wives or children of one's mother's brothers are not *sanak*, but *saudara*[6]; *saudara* being used of relationship on the paternal as well as on the maternal side.

Even when a woman's children marry, still they will reckon their parents-in-law only on the female side. *Minantu* means "son-in-law" or "daughter-in-law", both being equally recognized and valuable under the *'adat*. In Negri Sembilan *mintua* means "mother-in-law", but the phrase *bapa mintua*,

[1] If there are only three children the second is called *Ngah* (=Tengah) or *Achik*.
[2] *Mandeh ketē*, Min.
[3] *Dansanak, saudara samendeh*, Min.
[4] Her husband is called *tunadi*, Min.
[5] *Badansenak mandēh, b ibu* or *biai*.
[6] Sauskrit.

"father-in-law", is a neologism, the position not being included in the matriarchal conception of the family. For aunts and uncles-in-law one has not the brothers and sisters of one's bride's father, but those of her mother *mintua sanak ibu*.

Minangkabau custom recognizes no descent or relationship through males, but it has a term for the relationship of a father and a father's family to that of father's children. It calls them *orang babako* (Mal. *berbaka*). This nomenclature survives in the phrase *saka baka* used to express the origin of a person on both sides; *saka* describing the maternal, and *baka* the paternal side.

In Negri Sembilan the terms of relationship employed by the endogamous Malays of the other peninsular states are used to express relationship on the paternal side. The children of a man's sister[1] in Negri Sembilan are his *anak buah*, a phrase descriptive of descendants in the male line elsewhere but under the matriarchal constitution applied to a sister's children, because they alone are of the brother's own tribe: the children of a man's brother, a tie of relationship that did not concern the old matriarchy, are his *anak saudara*, his nephews and nieces in our sense of the word but nothing to him, seeing that they belong to their mother's tribe, a different tribe altogether. A maternal aunt is *emak sanak ibu*,[2] a paternal *emak saudara*. A maternal grand-aunt is *wan sanak ibu*; a maternal or paternal grandmother and paternal grand-aunts are simply *wan*. No distinction is drawn between uncles[3]; and both one's mother's brothers and one's father's brothers are *bapa saudara* or loosely *bapa*. Grandfathers[4] and grand-uncles, paternal and maternal, are all *to' aki*. Cousins on the male side are (*saudara*) *diri bapa*, as distinguished from *anak sanak ibu* those on one's mother's side. *Kadim*, an Arabic word, is used to denote close relationship alike on the distaff and on the male side.

With his passion for family trees, the Minangkabau Malay never omits to allude to any relationship established by marriage. *Ipar* is used of brother or sister-in-law on either side, that is, equally of brothers and sisters of the wife and of brothers and sisters of the husband: *ipar kadim* means a wife's or husband's full brother or sister; *ipar duai*, a husband's or wife's cousins; *abang ipar* means a brother-in-law older than self; *kakak ipar*, a sister-in-law older than self; and *adēk ipar*, a sister or brother-in-

---

[1] *Kamanakan kandong;* other descendants in the female line are his *Kamanakan*, or if remote his *anak buah:* he is their *mamak*.
[2] *Mandēh*.
[3] Maternal uncle = *mamak*, Min.
[4] Maternal grand-uncle = *mamak tuo kandong, mamak gaik*, remoter *'mak ninēk kendong, mamak moyang, mamak poyang*.

law younger than self.[1] The relationship between two men who have married sisters or two women who have married brothers[2] is known as *biras*: a man speaks of his *biras*, meaning the husband of his wife's sister, a woman of her *biras* meaning her husband's brother. The relationship established between parents whose children have intermarried is *bēsan*. If I and my wife are parents of one of the parties to a marriage and my friend and his wife to the other, we are *bēsan*: the father of the child who has married my child is my wife's *bēsan jantan* and the mother is my *bēsan betina*, and conversely. The relationship which exists between a husband and wife, both of whom have had a child by a former marriage is *bēsan sa-bantal*, if those children intermarry.

In all the states of the peninsula the marriage of first cousins is regarded with disfavour and is practised by hardly any Malays except the rajas.

[1] The sisters of a man's mother are his wife's *andan;* and his more distant female relations his *samandan* in Minangkabau.
[2] *Pambayan*, Min.

BIBLIOGRAPHY

JFMSM. = Journal of the Federated Malay States Museums.

JRAS. = Journal of the Royal Asiatic Society (London).

JRASMB. = Journal of the Royal Asiatic Society, Malayan Branch.

JRASSB. = Journal of the Royal Asiatic Society, Straits Branch.

I

The founder of Malay royalty and his conquest of Saktimuna the serpent, R. O. Winstedt, JRASMB., 1926; History of Negri Sembilan, R. O. Winstedt, *ib.*, 1943.

II

Prehistoric research in the Netherlands Indies (with a very full bibliography) R. Heine-Geldern, South-east Asia Institute, New York, 1945 (reprint from Science and Scientists in the Netherlands Indies); Prehistory in Malaya (with bibliography), M. W. F. Tweedie, JRAS., 1942; Pagan Races of the Malay Peninsula, W. W. Skeat and C. O. Blagden, London, 1906; Proceedings of the Third Congress of Prehistorians of the Far East, Singapore, 1940; Early Man, A. H. Brodrick, London, 1948; On slab-built graves in Perak, I. H. N. Evans, JFMSM., 1928, XII, pt. 3, p.119. The Bridge of the Dead, R. O. Winstedt, JRASMB., XXIV.

III

Pagan Races of the Malay Peninsula, W. W. Skeat and C. O. Blagden, London, 1906; Malay Magic, W. W. Skeat, 1900; The Malay Magician, R. O. Winstedt, London, 1951; Collected Papers on Analytical Psychology, C. G. Jung, London, 1920; History of Malaya, R. O. Winstedt, JRASMB., 1935; Malay Charms, R. O. Winstedt, JFMSM., Vol. IX, Pts. 2 (1920) and 4 (1922); Hinduism, Monier Williams,

1911, pp. 59, 60; Castes and Tribes of Southern India E. Thurston, Vol. I, *sub* Brahman; Archaeological Researches on ancient Indian colonization in Malaya, H. G. Quaritch-Wales, JRASMB., 1940; The Kelantan Shadow-play, Anker Rentse, *ib.*, 1936; Kingship and Enthronement in Malaya (with bibliography), R. O. Winstedt, JRAS., London, 1945; The Suma Oriental of Tomé Pires (Hakluyt Soc.), Vol. II, London, 1944; Islam To-day (Netherlands India and Malaya, R. O. Winstedt), ed. A. J. Arberry and Rom Landau, London, 1942; Malay Literature (with bibliography), R. O. Winstedt, JRASMB., 1940, Notes on Malay Magic, R. O. Winstedt, *ib.*, 1925; Jelebu Customary Songs and Sayings, A. Caldecott, JRASSB., LXXVIII; Muhammadan Mysticism in Sumatra, R. le Roy Archer, *ib.*, 1937; Samsu'l-din van Pasai, C. A. O. van Nieuwenhuijze, Leiden, 1945; The Itinerary of Ludovico di Varthema of Bologna from 1502 to 1508, London, 1928.

IV

Pagan Races of the Malay Peninsula, *ib.*; The Aboriginal Tribes, R. J. Wilkinson, Papers on Malay Subjects, Kuala Lumpur, 1910; The Ninety-Nine Laws of Perak, J. Rigby, *ib.*, 1908; Hindu Law and Custom, J. E. Jolly, Calcutta, 1928; Sejarah Melayu; Hikayat Sri Rama; Sumatra, E. M. Loeb, Vienna, 1935; Hindu Element in Malay Marriage Ceremony, R. O. Winstedt, JRASSB., LXXIX; Law and Customs of the Malays with reference to tenure of Land, Sir W. E. Maxwell, *ib.*, XII; Law relating to Slavery, W. E. Maxwell, *ib.*, XIII; 'adat Raja-Raja Melayu, Ph. van Ronkel, Leiden, 1929; Malay Family Law, E. N. Taylor, JRASMB., XV, 1937; Mother-right among Khassis and Malays, R. O. Winstedt, *ib.*, 1932; Negri Sembilan (with bibliography), R. O. Winstedt, *ib.*, 1934.

V

Sejarah Melayu; The Suma Oriental, T. Pires, 1944; Kingship and Enthronement in Malaya, R. O. Winstedt, JRAS., 1945; Oudheidkundig Verslag, Batavia, 1930 (Notices of books, R. O. W., JRASMB., 1932); Founder of

Malay royalty and his conquest of Saktimuna the Serpent, R. O. Winstedt, JRASMB., 1926; A History of Perak, *ib.*, 1943; History of Negri Sembilan, *ib.*; Kedah Laws, *ib.*, 1928; History of Pahang, W. Linehan, *ib.*, 1936; 'adat Raja-Raja Melayu, Ph. van Ronkel, Leiden.

VI

Jelebu Customary Songs and Sayings, A. Caldecott, JRASSB., LXXVIII; History of Rembau, C. W. C. Parr and W. H. Mackray, *ib.*, LVI; Customary Law of Rembau, and W. H. Mackray, *ib.*, LVI; Negri Sembilan, R. O. Winstedt, JRASMB., 1934; Customary Law of Rembau, E. N. Taylor, *ib.*, 1929; Malay Family Law, *ib.*, 1937; Divorce and Inheritance, E. N. Taylor, *ib.*, 1948; A Brunei Code, R. O. Winstedt, *ib.*, 1932; Kedah Laws, *ib.*, 1928; Risalat Hoekoem Kanoen (Undang-Undang Melaka), Ph. van Ronkel, Leiden, 1919; Hukum Kanun Pahang, ed. J. Kempe and R. O. Winstedt, JRASMB., XXI, 1948; Maritime Code of the Malays, Sir S. Raffles, JRASSB., 1879; The Johore Code, Journal of the Indian Archipelago, IX, 1855; Law, Pt. 1, R. J. Wilkinson, Papers on Malay Subjects, 1908; Ninety-Nine Laws of Perak, ed. J. Rigby, *ib.*, 1908; Old Malay Legal Digests and Malay Customary Law, R. O. Winstedt, JRAS., London, 1945; Handleidung bij de be ofening der Maleische Taal en Letterkunde, de Hollander, Breda, 1893.

VII

Political and Statistical Account of the British Settlements in the Straits of Malacca, T. S. Newbold, 2 vols., London, 1839; Pelayaran 'Abdullah, Singapore; A History of Malaya, R. O. Winstedt, 1935; Misa Melayu, ed. R. O. Winstedt, Singapore; In Malay Forests, W. G. Maxwell; Malay Industries, pt. II, Fishing, Hunting and Trapping, R. O. Winstedt, P.M.S., Kuala Lumpor, 1911; Malay Fisheries, Raymond Firth, London, 1946; Tomé Pires, *op. cit.*; Notes on Malay Archipelago and Malacca, W. P. Groeneveldt, Essays relating to Indo-China, 2nd series, vol. I; British Rule in Eastern Asia, L. A. Mills, London, 1942; Slab-

Graves and Iron Implements, R. O. Winstedt, JRASMB., 1941; Malacca Meridional India and Cathay, de Eredia, ed. J. V. Mills, *ib.*, 1930; A History of Pahang, W. Linehan, *ib.*, 1936; The Book of Duarte Barbosa, tr. by L. M. Dames, 2 vols., London, 1918 and 1921; Hikayat 'Abdullah; A New Account of the East Indies, Captain Alexander Hamilton; An Anecdotal History of Old Times in Singapore, C. B. Buckley, 2 vols., Singapore, 1902; Malaya's first British Pioneer (Francis Light), H. P. Clodd, London, 1948.

VIII

Malay Literature (with bibliography), R. O. Winstedt, JRASMB., XVII, 1940; The Panji Tales, *ib.*, 1941; A. Panji Tale from Kelantan, *lb.*, 1949.

IX

Prehistory in Malaya, M. W. F. Tweedie, JRAS., 1942; L'art Prebouddhique de la Chine et de l'Asie du Sud-Est et son influence en Oceanie, R. v. Heine-Geldern, Revue des Arts Asiatiques, T.XI, Paris, 1937; Indonesian Art (illustrated), a loan exhibition from the Royal Inidies Institute, Amsterdam, Introduction by R. v. Heine-Geldern, New York, 1948; Documents pour l'art comparé de l'Eurasie Septentrionale, A. Leroi-Gourhan, Paris, 1943; Bedeutung und Herkunft der Altestan Hinterindischen Metaltrommeln (Kesselgongs), R. v. Heine-Geldern, Asia Major, vol. VIII; L'age du bronze au Tonkin et dans le Nord-Annam, V. Goloubew, Bulletin de l'Ecole Française d'Extreme Orient, vol. XXIX; Archaeological Research in Indo-China, vol. I, fig. 4, O. R. T. Janse, Harvard, 1947; A History of Malaya, R. O. Winstedt, JRASMB., 1935, fig. 10; Malaya, ed. R. O. Winstedt, London, 1923, ills. pp. 110-5, 153-164; The Date of the Early Dong-so'n Culture, B. Karlgren, The Museum of Far Eastern Antiquities, Stockholm, No. 14, 1942; Reserches sur les Cambodgiens, G. Groslier, fig. 55; Le Cambodge, E. Aymonier, I, fig. 9; Les 'Tissus a jonques' du sud de Sumatra, A. Steinmann, Revue des Arts Asiatiques, T. XI, Paris, 1937; A Motif in Indonesian Art, R. O. Winstedt, JRAS., pts. 3 and 4, 1944, pp. 130-2; The Art of the Northern Nomads (with bibliography), E. H. Mins, Proceedings of the British Academy, vol. XXVIII, 1942; Proceedings of the Third Congress of Prehistorians of the Far East; Some Weapons and Tools of the Yin dynasty, B. Karlgren, *op. cit.*, No. 17, 1945; Über Kris-Griffe und ihre mythischen Grundlagen, R. v. Heine-Geldern, Ostasiatische Zeitschrift, Berlin, 1932; Keris and other Malay Weapons, G. B. Gardner, Singapore, 1936; A. Note on the Kingfisher *Kĕris*, I. H. N. Evans, JFMSM., vol. XV, 1932; Archaeological Researches, H. G. Quaritch-Wales, JRASMB., XVIII, 1940; Gold Ornaments dug up at Fort Canning, R. O. Winstedt, *ib.*, 1928; Oriental Silverwork (Malay and Chinese), H. Ling Roth, London, 1910; De l'origine commune des linteaux de l'Inde Pallava et des linteaux Khmers préangkoriens, G. de Coral Remusat, Revue des Arts Asiatiques, T. VIII, Paris, 1934; Art and Thought, ed. K. Bharata Iyer (pp. 66–7), Tibetan Book Covers, G. Tucci, London, 1947; Pictorial History of Civilization in Java, W. F. Stutterheim, Weltevreden; West-Indonesian, A. Kramer, Stuttgart; Sumatra, E. M. Loeb (with chapter by R. v. Heine-Geldern), Vienna, 1935; Forgotten Kingdoms in Sumatra, F. M. Schnitger, Leiden, 1939; Malay Industries, Pt. I, Arts and Crafts, R. O. Winstedt, Papers on Malay Subjects, Kuala Lumpur, 1909; Histories of Malaya, Johor and Perak (plates), R. O. Winstedt, JRASMB. The Stone Age of Indonesia, H. K. van Heekeren, Verhandelingen van het Koninklijk Inst. voor Taal-, Land-en Volkenkunde, Deel XXI, The Bronze Age of Indonesia, *ib.* Deel XXII; The Stone Age in Malaya, M. W. F. Tweedie, JRASMB, vol. XXVI, Pt. 2, 1953; Das Tocharerproblem und die Pontische Wanderung, R. v. Heine-Geldern, Saeculum II, 1951; Prehistoric Life in Indonesia, H. R. v. Heekeren, Djakarta, 1955.

INDEX

Aborigines of Malaya, 7–15, 18, 45, 63, 122, 124, 164
Acheh, 38–40, 49, 80
Administration, Malay; matriarchal, 81–90; patriarchal, 63–81
Agriculture, 124–7
Alexander the Great, 2, 36–7, 70, 145
Anarchy in Malay States, 120
Animism, 7, 19–20
Arabs, sacrifice by, 23
Arabic, literature from Egypt, 153; learning Kuran in, 177
Art, Dong-so'n, 9, 10, 161–6, 169; Indian, 166–173; Javanese, 172; Malay, 161–175; megalithic, 161; Mycenaean, 162; Pala, 171; of steppes, 161
Assyrio-Babylonian influence, 2, 32, 64
Atharva-Veda, incantation from, 32
Australo-Melanesoids, 6–8

Batak art, 9; horse sacrifice, 29; slaves, 53
British influence, on Malay life, 3, 43, 176–8; on administration, 80, 81, 90; on law, 99, 107, 117; on economics, 123, 125–6, 134–5
Bronze Age in Malaya, 161, 165
Buddhism, traces of in Malaya; images, 26, 27, 130; enthronement ritual, 66, 67; Tibetan, 149; creese-hilts, 166–8; silver patterns, 171, 173
Bugis immigrants, 49, 133; maritime laws for, 118; weapons, 165, 167
Burial, methods of, 12, 13, 20, 24, 29

Chams, 129
Chinese, miners, 129, 131; faction fights, 178; in Malayan politics, 179, and trade, 136–8; as versifiers, 157
Communism, Minangkabau tribal, 136

Confucius, 67
Copra, 127
Creese, the, 165–8

Dayaks, 7, 9, 13, 23, 24, 64, 162
Dong-so'n v. Art.
Dutch, influence on Malays, 43; at Malacca, 73, 102

Elephants, trade in, 121
Enthronement ritual, 65–8

Family, the Malay; matriarchal, 56–62; patriarchal, 45–50
Fishing industry, 122–4

Gold-mining, 129

Hamzah of Barus, 27, 35, 39, 148–9, 156
Hindu influence, 14, 26–33, 35, 45–8, 51–4, 63–9, 74–5, 88, 91, 99–102, 105–6, 110–2, 116, 122, 134, 139–142, 166–9, 171

Indian influence, on administration, 76; beliefs, 36–7; crafts, 170, 174; law, 116; literature, 134
Indonesia, 3, 4
Iron tools, 164

Jakun v. Aborigines
Java and Javanese influence, 23, 26–7, 29, 33, 35, 43, 51, 66, 68, 140, 142–4
Johor, 16, 26, 72–3, 79, 87, 124, 128

Kedah, 6, 26, 31, 41, 50, 80, 117, 125, 137

Lampong textiles, 162–3
Land laws, Malay, 109–111, 114–6
Language, the Malay, 16–7

INDEX

Law, Malay digests of, 91–2; maritime, 118; matriarchal, 92–99; patriarchal, 99–118; Johor, 119; Kedah, 110, 116; Malacca, 99–105, 112; Pahang, 102–5, 108–9, 112–3; Perak, 52, 56, 103–6, 109, 111–2, 114
Light, Francis, 16, 133
Literature, Malay, 139–160

Magic, Hindu, 31; Perak, 79; Semitic, 32; Sufi, 41
Mahabharata, 30, 142
Malacca, 15, 20, 29, 34, 38, 46, 49–52, 68–77, 85, 91, 94, 99–102, 121, 126, 128, 134
Malay Annals, 150–1
Malay class distinctions, 50–2; culture, 2–3, 176–9, 181; family 48–9; marriage, 45–8; race, 15; women, 44, 49–50
Malays, agricultural and maritime, 16
Marco Polo, 38
Marketing, 131
Marriage, Malay, 45–8
Matriarchy in Negri Sembilan, 48, 51, 57–62, 81–90, 92–9
Melanesians, 19
Meru, Mount, 67, 69
Minangkabau culture, 2, 66; matriarchy, 48, 51, 57–62, 81–90, 92–9
Mining, gold, 129; tin, 129–131
Mois, 12, 18, 53
Muhammadanism, 2, 3, 33–44, 46; influence of, on administration, 79, on art, 173, 181; on law, 91–2, 100–9, 111–8, on literature, 144–151; on society, 1, 46–8, 52

Negri Sembilan v. Minangkabau
Negritos v. Aborigines

Pahang, 6, 10, 68, 73, 77, 79, 124, 128, 130
Pasai, 33–4, 38–9, 51, 124, 151, 155
Penang, 16
Perak, 5, 6, 10, 21, 26, 36, 37, 48, 49, 54, 68–77, 129, 130, 134

Pires, T., 33–5, 46, 63, 76–7, 108, 129, 130, 132–4
Pottery, 174–5
Prehistory, 5–7

Rajas, Malay, 50–2; as traders, 132–3
Ramayana, 30, 37, 74, 140, 142, 151, 165–6, 173
Rice-planting, 124–6
Rubber industry, 127
Rulers, Malay, 2, 44, 45, 86–8, 132–3

Sacrifice, 21–3, 27, 29, 53
Sakai v. Aborigines
Sanskrit, 139–140, 169
Senoi v. Aborigines
Shadow-play, 30, 36, 146
Shamanism, 23–5, 27
Shams al-din, 39, 40
Silver-work, 171–3
Slavery, 52–6
Spectre Huntsman, 1–2, 14
Spirits, 20–1, 23
Steppes, art of, 161
Stone-age, 5–7, 161
Sufism, 25, 35, 38–44
Sumba, 162–4

Tantrism, 27, 66, 171
Textiles, 162–4, 169, 170
Thousand Questions, Book of, 149
Tin-mining, 129–131
Titles, Malay; patriarchal, 50–52, 70–7; matriarchal, 82–4, 86
Torajas, 1, 6
Trengganu, 27, 34, 80, 107

Upanishad, Katha, 148
Verse, Malay, 153–160
Vijaya, Sri, 26, 67, 69, 70, 76, 125, 169

Wahhabis, 42–3
Weapons, 165–8

Yues, 161
Yun-nan, 2, 13, 157, 162

For Product Safety Concerns and Information please contact our EU
representative GPSR@taylorandfrancis.com
Taylor & Francis Verlag GmbH, Kaufingerstraße 24, 80331 München, Germany

www.ingramcontent.com/pod-product-compliance
Lightning Source LLC
Chambersburg PA
CBHW061444300426
44114CB00014B/1824